Poor communication cost you money
The power of job-specific terms in your hands!

# SPANISH
## DICTIONARY

*for*

# CONTRACTORS

by
**Joseph L. Colclough**
**Seamless Solutions, LLC**

## EASY - POWERFUL - EFFECTIVE

**Library of Congress Cataloging-in-Publication Data**

Colclough, Joseph L.
Spanish Dictionary for
Contractors/Joseph L. Colclough
   cs. fc. – (for contractors)

ISBN 978-0615757636 (Seamless
Solutions, LLC.)
        Spanish language-Construction
        Contruction-Terminology
        Business Spanish-Contractors

## About the Author

Joseph L. Colclough is an innovative teacher, speaker and entrepreneurial businessman. He holds a Bachelor's Degree in Psychology from University of Massachusetts at Amherst, a Masters Degree in Education with a minor in Spanish from State University of New York at New Paltz.

Colclough taught secondary school foreign language classes for over ten years and has traveled to: Guayaquil, Ecuador; Ensenada, Mexico; San Juan, Puerto Rico and Seville, Spain

.

In the construction industry he has served for over 15 years, and his entrepreneurial spirit led him to form the New York based corporation called Seamless Solutions, LLC. You will find his writing style to be both informative and easy applicable to real-life situations.

# TABLE OF CONTENTS

**RESOURCE GUIDE:**

**DICTIONARY:**

# I. Alphabet

# Alphabet (el alfabeto)

Effective communication in Spanish starts with correct pronunciation. Correct pronunciation starts with mastering the Spanish alphabet. Mastering the Spanish alphabet starts with practice. The good news is that there are far fewer exceptions in the Spanish language than in the English language.

# The old adage rightly states: "Spanish is read the way that it is said".

On your journey to discover the Spanish language, the Spanish alphabet is a good first step. As you take some time to discover and practice the Spanish alphabet, you will find yourself miles ahead on the road of good pronunciation. Don't get bogged down with cumbersome phonetics. Grow the power of bilingual communication in your own hands.

HOT TIP!

The Spanish alphabet originally had 30 letters and still does according to many Latin American countries. The letters (ch, ll, rr) were eliminated from the Spanish alphabet in 1994 according to the Spanish language authority, *Real Academia* Española. The Real Academia of Spain eliminated the

"CH, "LL", and "RR" as separate letters and only the "Ñ" remains, making the official total to be 27 letters.

However, if you are not online and want to look up a word in a Spanish dictionary, the old letters are often still found their original listings. For example, if you are searching for the word "lluvia" and it is nowhere to be found in the "L" section of the dictionary. Try looking in the "LL" section of the dictionary and you might land a hat full of luck.

| Letra (letter) | Nombre (name) | Sonido (sound) |
|---|---|---|
| A | A | ah |
| B | Be | bay |
| C | Ce | say |
| *CH | Che | chay |
| D | De | day |
| E | E | ay |
| F | Efe | EF-fay |
| G | Ge | hay |
| H | Hache *h is silent.. | AH-chay |

| I | I | ee |
|---|---|---|
| J | Jota "J" is pronounced like an English "h" | HOH-ta |
| K | Ka | kah |
| L | Ele | EL-ay |
| *LL | Elle (eyeh) | AY-yay |
| M | Eme | EM-ay |
| N | Ene | EN-ay |
| Ñ | Eñe | EN-yay |
| O | O | oh |
| P | Pe | pay |
| Q | Qu | koo |
| R | Ere | ER-ay |
| **RR** | Erre | ERR-ay |
| S | Ese | EH-say |
| T | Te | tay |
| U | U | oo |
| V | Ve | bvay |
| W | Doble ve | DOUGH-blay-bay |
| X | Equis | EH-keys |
| Y | i griega | EE-gree-AY-gah |
| Z | Zeta | SAY-tah |

# need some practice?

Say you hire Pedro Montillo and need to write down the correct spelling of his last name along with his driver's licence number (numbers are next chapter). Try spelling the last names listed below. Use the chart above, and make it your goal to be able to say the correct "sound" of each "letter". Focus on the "sound" or "sonido" column for practice and when you feel like you got it, cover up the **"sonido"** column and try spelling!

## HOT TIP!

Accent marks are only found on vowels in Spanish. Just say the name of the letter in Spanish and then add "con acento" after it, if the letter has an accent.

For example, if you wanted to say the letter "o" has an accent (ó) you would say "o" con acento.

| | |
|---|---|
| Paniego | Herrada |
| Rodríguez | López |
| Benavidez | Moreno |
| Gutiérrez | Sabater |
| Montilla | González |
| Carrasqueo | Hernández |
| Alfonso | García |

## HOT TIP!

**When a good singer sings, the power behind the sound comes from the CHEST. Similarly, when you pronounce Spanish words or letters, let the sound come from your chest rather than relying so heavily on your nose and mouth. Sound crazy? Give it a try and you will see the difference yourself.**

# II. Pronunciation Guide

Watch out!  There is a natural tendency to rely on phonetics when attempting to pronounce words in a foreign language.

Cumbersome phonetics can actually slow you down!  It is better to learn HOW to pronounce Spanish words correcty from the start.

Get ready to dive into your new journey of good pronunciation and watch the power of language grow in your own hands!

You will find that in this book, the use of phonetics have been kept to a mininum for the very reason that they will inhibit your ability to master good pronounce skills in Spanish. Good pronunciation is the very foundation upon which language is built.

# Pronunciaton Guide

| Letter & /Sound/ | Explanation | Examples |
|---|---|---|
| a,e,i,o,u /same as English/ | *For a more authentic sound with Spanish vowels be consise when sounding them out.*<br><br>Don't' say "CAAASAAA" but "CASA". Be short and discrete when sounding out the vowels. Practice of few of the examples. | casa, coco, Lola, mono |
| b, v /b/ | *The "b" and the "v" are pronounced slightly different in Spanish. Pronounce the "b" like the English "b". Pronounce the "v" like a "bv" in English and don't let your lips go forward when you pronounce it.* | vaso, beso, vino, Bogotá |
| ca,co,cu | *In combination* | casa, Colombia, |

| /k/ | with a,o,u its sounds /k/. | Cuba, Caribe |
|---|---|---|
| ce, ci /s/ | The "c" used with "e" or "i" sounds like an "s" in most Latinamerican countries. | Cecilia, cenar, cima |
| ch /tsch/ | The "ch" sounds like "tsch" | Chile, chica, chocolate |
| ga, go, gu /g/ | The "g" sounds just like the English "g" when used with "a", "o" or "u". | gato, gustar, gota |
| ge, gi /h/ | G in combination with "e" or "i" sounds like an "h". | Guibraltar, gente |
| gue, gui /ge/, /gi/ | The combination "gue" sounds like "gay" and "gui" sounds like "giy" | guerrero, guerra, guitarra |
| güe, güi /gue/, /gui/ | When you see the two dots over the "u" it means that u IS pronounced. | pingüino, antigüedad |
| H | h is silent. | hola, Honduras, Habana |
| j /h/ | The "j" has the same "h" sound with all vowels. | Javier, José, Juan, |
| ll /y/ | The "ll" is prounounced | Mallorca, yeso, lluvia |

| | | |
|---|---|---|
| | differently depending on the nationality of the speaker. The general rule of thumb is to pronounce it *like the English "y"*. | |
| ñ /n+y/ | Think NY! Sounds like the "ny" in canyon. | Niño, señor, español |
| que, qui /k/ | *Sounds like "k". Exists only in the combinations "qui" or "que"* | quién, que, queso |
| r, rr | *If you can't roll or trill your tongue just extend the "r" sound longer "rrrrrr".* | ratón, carro, perro caro, pero |
| x /ks/ | *Like English "ks".* | anexo |
| za, zo, zu /s/ | *Same sound like ce and ci.* | zapato, zorro, Zulia |

# III. Culture Guide

Culture is the context of language. It is good to have an understanding of cultural basics before you begin to use the language.

This will make you a powerful and effective communicator with credibility and impact.

**Watch the power of language go to work!**

# Using the right "you" in Spanish.

Deeply set in the Hispanic (pertaining to Latin America) and Spanish (pertaining to Spain) culture is the concept of respect. The modern term "usted" was originally the term "vuestra merced". This expression "vuestra merced" can be translated as "your grace".

Historically, Spain was made up of separate class structures, creating a socio-economic division between weathy nobles and the common people.

Common people were required to address nobles in a respectful manner. Respectful terms such as "your grace" or "vuestra merced" were commonly used. If a commoner failed to show proper respect, a nobleman had full license to take out his sword and remove that common person's head.

As a result, terms of respect became essential elements in all social exchanges.

The term "vuestra merced", abbreviated as Vd., changed over time to become the word "usted". "Usted" is abbreviated as Ud., and continues to be used today in modern culture.

Since there are four ways of saying "you" in Spanish, it is important to know which one to use in each situation. It is a common yet avoidable mistake, to use the wrong "you".

In the workplace informal settings are next to none since the workplace is considered to be a professional setting.

Informal seetings are reserved for friends, family and close aquaintances.

For informal settings, when addressing an individual, the word "Tú" is used to say "you". However, in all other social and professional settings, use the "usted" form in order to properly address another person.

## HOT TIP!

**Since the workplace is considered to be a professional setting, stick with the "usted" form; or "ustedes" form, if you are addressing two or more workers at the same time.**

# The slang term "gringo".

You might have heard the word "gringo" in conversation. What does it mean? "Gringo" can be literally translated "Yankee" in the noun form or "unitelligable", in the adjective form.

The origin of the term "Gringo" is ambiguous. According to folklore, the term came about due to the unwanted presence of American soldiers at the Mexican border. These soldiers were easily identified by their green uniforms and thus the term "green go" became, to the Spanish-speaker, the word "gringo". Over time this slang term has been used to describe a "Yankee / North American" **OR** a North American speaking "unintelligible" Spanish. When the term is used to soley refer to a person as a North American, it is not meant to be derogatory. When used to say that someone speaks unintelligible Spanish, then it is used in a derogatory fashion.

Take it or leave it, you will hear this word used. If one of your workers calls you a 'gringo', don't be offended, just set the tone and remind the worker: **"I'm the boss, you are not" "Soy el patrón que usted no es"**.
Or, "Leave the comedy for the comedy club" "Deje la comedia en el club de la comedia".
Otherwise, if you prefer a more extreme solution: "You're fired!", "-> *¡queda despedido!*".

# IV. Expressions

**ON THE JOB EXPRESSIONS**

- **Greetings & Farewells**
- **Useful Spanish Expressions**
- **Key Spanish Expressions**

# *Greetings & Farewells*

| | |
|---|---|
| **Good morning!** | **¡Buenos días!** |
| **Good afternoon!** | **¡Buenas tardes!** |
| **Good evening! Good night!** | **¡Buenas noches!** |
| **Hello!** | **¡Hola!** |
| **See you later!** | **¡Hasta luego!** |
| **See you tomorrow!** | **¡Hasta mañana!** |

# Useful Spanish Expressions

| | |
|---|---|
| Please. | Por favor. |
| Thank you. | Gracias. |
| You're welcome. | De nada. |
| Excuse me | Disculpe |
| I need to see your driver's license? | Necesito ver su licencia de conductores. |
| How many years experience do you have in this profession? | ¿Cuántos años de experiencia tiene en esta profesión? |

| | |
|---|---|
| This job pays ($8,$9,$10,$11,$12,$13,$14) an hour. | Este trabajo se paga (ocho, nueve, diez, once, doce, trece, catorce) dólares por hora. |

# Key Expressions

| | |
|---|---|
| Excuse me, sir. | Perdón, señor. |
| Ma'am. | Señora. |
| Miss/Ms. | Señorita. |
| Do you speak English? | ¿Habla inglés? |
| Yes | Sí. |
| No. | No. |
| I don't speak a lot (of Spanish). Pay attention and listen to my instructions. | No hablo mucho (español). Preste atención y escuche mis instrucciones. |
| If you don't follow instructions, I will fire you. | Si no sigue instrucciones, le despediré. |
| Speak slower | Hable más |

| | |
|---|---|
| please. | despacio por favor. |
| Please repeat. | Repita por favor. |
| May I ask you a question? | ¿Puedo hacerle una pregunta? |
| Help me with this, right away. | Ayúdeme con esto, en seguida. |
| I'm the boss you are not. | Soy el patrón que usted no es. |
| A quality job is the only job we do. | Un trabajo de calidad es el único trabajo que hacemos. |
| If you break it, you buy it. | Si se le rompe, lo compra. |
| Treat all of the customer's property and personal belongings with respect. | Respete todas pertenencias y efectos personales del cliente. |

| | |
|---|---|
| Don't be careless. Put all tools back where they belong. | No seas una persona descuidada. Coloque las herramientas en su lugar correcto. |
| Pick up the pace or go home. | Apúrense o váyase a casa. |

# V.  NUMBERS

**Everything you need know to use numbers in Spanish effectively on the job.**

- **Knowing your numbers**
- **Measurements**
- **NumbersGrammar Camp**
- **Stating & telling time. [Tell your workers when to show up, break for lunch or go home!]**

| | |
|---|---|
| 1 uno | 21 veintiuno |
| 2 dos | 22 veintidós |
| 3 tres | 23 veintitrés |
| 4 cuatro | 24 veinticuatro |
| 5 cinco | 25 veinticinco |
| 6 seis | 26 veintiséis |
| 7 siete | 27 veintisiete |
| 8 ocho | 28 veintiocho |
| 9 nueve | 29 veintinueve |
| 10 diez | 30 treinta |
| | |
| 11 once | 31 treinta y uno |
| 12 doce | 32 treinta y dos |
| 13 trece | 33 treinta y tres..... |
| 14 catorce | |
| 15 quince | 40 cuarenta |
| 16 dieciséis | |
| 17 diecisiete | 50 cincuenta |
| 18 dieciocho | 60 sesenta |
| 19 diecinueve | 70 setenta |
| 20 veinte | 80 ochenta |
| | 90 noventa |
| | |
| | 100 cien |
| | |
| | 1000 mil |
| | |
| | 1.000.000 un millón |

**HOT TIP!**

If you want to tell Paco to cut **a piece** that is **100 inches long**, say "**Córtela a cien pulgadas**".

# Measurements

| Inches | Pulgadas |
|---|---|
| Feet | Pies |
| 1/16 | Un dieciseisavo |
| 1/8 | Un octavo |
| ¼ | Un cuarto |
| ½ | Media (pulgada) |
| ¾ | Tres cuartos |
| 3' 8½" | es pies ocho y media pulgadas |

**Cut me a piece that is 48" x 59".**

**Córteme una pieza de cuarenta y ocho pulgadas por cincuenta y nueve pulgadas.**

# Spanish Measurements

| Spanish | English | Length in feet |
|---------|---------|----------------|
| pulgada | "inch" | $\frac{1}{12}$ |
| pie | "foot" | 1 |
| vara | "yard" | 3 |
| paso | "pace" | 5 |
| legua | "league" | 15,000 |

# NUMBERS GRAMMAR CAMP

### THE 100 RULE!

There are two ways of saying **100** in Spanish **"cien"** or **"ciento".** When using 100 before a noun USE "CIEN". THIS IS ONLY FOR THE EXACT NUMBER 100 NOT FOR 101, 102, 103 ETC.

## EXAMPLES!

100 hammers – cien martillos

100 screws -      cien tornillos

100 nails-        cien clavos

100 dollars -     cien dólares

## 101-199 RULE!

For numbers **101-199** use "CIENTO".

(101) **ciento uno**

(102) **ciento dos**

(113) ciento trece.

Even if you add a noun, it is still "CIENTO".

**(102 BOSSES) ciento dos patrones**

**(113 SAWS) ciento trece sierras.**

## WATCH OUT FOR ONE "UNO"!

"Uno" changes to **"un"** before a
**masculine noun**

**uno → un**

"Uno" changes to **"una"** before a **femenine noun.**

**uno → una**

## For example:

Ex) (101 MANAGERS) ciento un gerentes

(201 TRUCKS)    doscientos y una camiones

(301 ROOMS)    trescientos y una habitaciones

**100 cien, 101 ciento uno, etc...**

**200 doscientos, doscientas**
**300 trescientos, trescientas**
**400 cuatrocientos, cuatrocientas**

**500 quinientos, quinientas**
**600 seiscientos, seiscientas**
**700 setecientos, setecientas**
**800 ochocientos, ochocientas**
**900 novecientos, novecientas**

## Watch out for 500, 700, 900!

# HOT TIP!

If the hundred numbers refer to a **femenine noun** then they will change from **–os** to **–as**.

**For example:**

(200 oranges) doscient**as** naranj**as**.

(500 spades)  quinient**as** pal**as**

(700 ladders) setecient**as** escaler**as**

# HOT TIP!

> **Larger numbers are built on the foundation of smaller numbers. Master the smaller units and you will master the larger ones.**

1000 mil
2000 dos mil
35.000 treinta y cinco mil, etc.

1973 = mil novecientos setenta y tres

> **In Spanish the use of the decimal point and the comma are REVERSED.**

| English | Spanish |
|---------|---------|
| 1.35 | 1,35 |
| 9.87 | 9,87 |
| 35,000 | 35.000 |
| 1,000,000 | 1.000.000 (un millón) |

# STATING & TELLING TIME

## Quick Reference Chart:

| | |
|---|---|
| What time is it? | ¿Qué hora es? |
| What time does the job start today? | ¿A qué hora comienza el trabajo hoy? |
| Report to work at (5,6,7,8,9) a.m. **sharp** tomorrow morning. | Preséntese a trabajar a las (cinco, seis, siete, ocho, nueve) **en punto** mañana. |
| At 5 p.m. | A las cinco de la tarde. |
| At 1:15. | A la una y cuarto. |
| At 1:30. | A la una y media. |
| At 1:45 | A las dos menos cuarto. |
| At midnight. | A la medianoche. |
| At noon. | Al mediodía. |
| Five minutes ago. | Hace cinco |

| | minutos. |
|---|---|
| After 8 pm | Después de las ocho de la noche. |
| Before 9 am. | Antes de las nueve de la mañana. |
| I expect you to show up for work on time. Plan ahead, no Excuses. | Espero que se presente al trabajo a tiempo. Haga un plan con anticipación, no hay Excusas. |
| Early | Temprano |
| Late | Tarde |

1800+ TRANSLATIONS

# ENGLISH TO SPANISH

EASY REFERENCE

# DICTIONARY

1800+
TRANSLATIONS

# ENGLISH → SPANISH DICTIONARY

| | |
|---|---|
| **abatement** | corrección [ko-rek-SYON] |
| **abatement period** | periodo de corrección [per-YO-do de ko-rek-SYON] |
| **above grade** | sobre tierra, sobre el nivel |
| **abrasive blasting** | limpieza a presión con abrasivos |
| **abrasive blasting enclosure** | espacio cerrado para limpieza a presión con abrasivos |
| **abut (to)** | ensamblar |
| **action level** | nivel de acción |

| | |
|---|---|
| **adapter** | adaptador |
| **addenda** | apéndice, adiciones, añadiduras |
| **addition (building)** | ampliación |
| **address** | dirección [di-rek-SYON], domicilio [do-mi-SIL-yo] |
| **adhesive** | adhesiva |
| **A-frame** | techo inclinado |
| **aggregate** | conglomerado, agregado |
| **air** | aire [AY-ray] |
| **air conditioning** | aire acondicionado |
| **-a/c central** | aire acondicionado central |
| **-a/c wall unit** | aparato de aire acondicionado |
| **air purifying respirator** | equipo de respiración purificador de aire |
| **air receiver** | depósito de aire comprimido |
| **airborne concentration** | concentración de partículas suspendida en el aire |
| **Allen (adjustable) wrench** | llave Inglesa |
| **Allen key** | llave Allen |
| **aluminum** | aluminio |
| **anchor** | anclaje |
| **anchor bolts** | pernos de anclaje |

| | |
|---|---|
| **anchorage** | anclaje |
| **angle** | angular |
| **angulated roping** | sistema de suspensión en ángulo |
| **anhydrous ammonia** | amoníaco anhidro |
| **appeal** | apelar [a-pel-AR] |
| **appliance** | electrodoméstico, aparato |
| **approve** | aprobar [a-pro-BAR] |
| **approved impact valve** | válvula aprobada resistente a impacto |
| **appurtenant** | anexo, que pertenece a |
| **artifacts** | altera los tejidos, artefactos |
| **asbestos** | asbesto |
| **asbestos dust** | polvo de asbesto |
| **asphalt** | asfalto |
| **atmospheric tank** | tanque a presión atmosférica |
| **attachment cap** | clavija de conexión |
| **attrition** | desgaste |
| **auger-bit** | gusanillo de taladro |
| **authorize** | autorizar [auw-to-ri-SAR] |
| **autoclaved cotton** | algodón esterilizado en el autoclave |
| **automatic overload device** | dispositivo automático de sobrecarga |

| | |
|---|---|
| automatic quick-closing coupling | acoplador automático de cierre rápido |
| automatic sprinkler system | sistema automático rociador |
| auxiliary self contained breathing apparatus | equipo de respiración auxiliar auto-contenido |
| aviation snips | tijeras de aviación |
| A-weighted sound level | nivel de sonido medido en la escala A |
| awl | lezna |
| B- organic vapor gas mask chin - style | B- para vapores gaseosos orgánicos tipo barbilla |
| back pressure check valve | válvulas para la contrapresión |
| back siphonage | sifones |
| back welded | terminar con soldadura |
| back-flow check valve | válvula de retención de flujo en retroceso |
| backhoe | excavador trasera |
| baffle | deflector |
| baffle type hoopers | tolvas deflectoras |
| bag-arm elevator | palanca elevadora de costales |
| balance | balanza |
| bale | bala |
| ball bearing block | motón de caja de bolas |

| | |
|---|---|
| baluster | balaustres |
| band center frequency in cycles per second | frecuencia de banda central en ciclos por segundo |
| barrel | barril giratorio |
| barrier | barrera |
| baseboard | zócalo |
| basket | canasta |
| batch type generator | generador intermitente |
| bathtub | bañera, tina |
| batt | pieza de tela |
| battery | batería |
| beam | viga, travesaño |
| beam head | plato del plegador |
| beam type platform | plataforma de viga |
| bearer | soporte |
| bearing block | bloque de apoyo |
| belt sander | lijadora de banda |
| belt-feed device | dispositivo alimentador de correa |
| bench stand machine | máquina con soporte de piso |
| benchman, coke side | artesano de banco, del lado del horno de coque |
| benchman, pusher side | artesano del banco, del lado de empuje |
| benzin (benzine) | bencina |
| billet shears | cizalles para |

| | lingotes |
|---|---|
| **binder** | aglutinante |
| **bins** | tolva, bandeja, recipiente, caja, barril |
| **bite** | punto de agarre |
| **black steel** | acero sin galvanizar |
| **blacksmith hammer** | martillo de mano para forjar, destajador |
| **blade** | cuchilla |
| **blade guide rod** | barra guía cuchilla |
| **blade shank** | cuchilla |
| **blast cleaning barrel** | tonel giratorio |
| **blast hole** | barreno de detonación |
| **blasting agent** | agente detonante |
| **blasting cap** | casquillo detonador (fulminante) |
| **block (of wood)** | tarugo, zoquete |
| **blow down** | soplar |
| **blow pit** | foso para el producto digerido |
| **blower** | ventilador |
| **blowers** | sopladores, ventiladores, |
| **board** | plancha |
| **board (drop) hammer** | martinete de caída libre con plancha de madera |
| **boatswain's chair scaffold** | andamio de silla mecedora |

| | |
|---|---|
| **body and fender work** | trabajo de hojalatería |
| **body harness** | arnés del cuerpo |
| **boiler** | calentador de agua |
| **boilover** | sobrecalentamiento |
| **bolster** | travesaño |
| **bolster plate** | placa porta-estampa |
| **bolts** | tornillo, perno |
| **bond wire** | alambre de conexión |
| **bonding** | amarre |
| **bonding agent** | agente de enlace |
| **boom** | armadía, brazo de grúa |
| **boom men** | encargados de la armadía |
| **booster cutoff** | cierre para la bomba reforzadora de presión |
| **booster pump** | bomba reforzadora de presión |
| **boot pulley** | polea inferior |
| **boring** | taladrar |
| **bottom plate** | solera inferior |
| **bowl** | tazón |
| **bowline knot** | nudo de presilla |
| **brace** | riostra, amarre |
| **bracing** | andamiaje, anclaje |
| **bracing** | tirantes |
| **bracket** | palometa |
| **brackets** | soportes |
| **brake** | freno |

| | |
|---|---|
| **brake locks** | cinta del freno |
| **brazed-brass** | soldadura dura de bronce |
| **brazing** | soldadura dura |
| **breaching parts** | piezas de cierre |
| **break (lunch)** | descanso |
| **breakdown** | voltaje disruptivo |
| **breaker** | interruptor automático |
| **breaker panel** | panel de interruptores automáticos |
| **breast derrick** | cabria de parapeto |
| **breast plate** | placa pectoral |
| **breathing zone** | zona de respiración |
| **breathing zone height** | altura de la zona de respiración |
| **breathlessness** | sin aire, respiración entrecortada |
| **brick** | ladrillo |
| **bricklayer's square scaffold** | andamio con base cuadrada para albañiles |
| **brow log** | tronco protector |
| **brush (cleaning)** | cepillo |
| **brush (painting)** | brocha |
| **bucket** | cubeta |
| **bucket elevator** | canasto para elevar, elevador de cangilones |
| **budging fuses** | puentear los fusibles |

| | |
|---|---|
| **buff** | pulir, lijar |
| **building** | edificio |
| **building code** | código de construcción |
| **building face rollers** | rodillo para la cara del edificio |
| **bulk head** | resguardo de contención, dique |
| **bulk terminal** | terminales de carga a granel |
| **bulldozer** | niveladora |
| **bult** | cabo de mecha |
| **bumber block** | calzo para choques |
| **bungs** | boca |
| **bunk block** | cuña tipo travesaño |
| **burner** | quemador |
| **burns** | cenizas |
| **burr** | rebaba |
| **bush** | arbusto |
| **bushed block** | motón encasquillado |
| **bushing** | anillo de reducción |
| **bypassing** | paso alterno, sin interferir con |
| **C- organic vapor gas mask canister front or back mounted** | C- cartucho para vapores gaseosos orgánicos colocada en el pecho o sobre la espalda |
| **cabinet** | gabinete |
| **cable** | cable |
| **caissons** | cámaras de aire |

| | comprimido |
|---|---|
| **caked oxidizers** | oxidantes aglutinados |
| **calenders** | calandrias, máquina para dar brillo (lustre) a telas, papel, etc. (material pasa entre dos rodillos) |
| **calibration point** | punto de calibración |
| **calibration sampling train** | tren de calibración para tomar muestra |
| **caliper** | calibrador |
| **calk gun** | pistola de calafateo/selladora |
| **call numbers** | servicios de llamada |
| **can** | lata |
| **can coining** | forjado de latas a medidas exactas |
| **can opener** | abrelatas |
| **canister** | cartuchos |
| **canopy hood** | campana de techo |
| **cap** | tapa |
| **capacitor welding** | soldadura por condensador |
| **capture velocity** | velocidad de captura |
| **carboy** | garrafón |
| **carboy tilter** | dispositivo volcadura del recipiente para electrolitos |

| | |
|---|---|
| **card** | cardar |
| **carpenters bracket scaffold** | andamio de palometas para carpintero, andamio con soportes para carpinteros |
| **carpet** | alfombra |
| **carpet stretcher** | estirador de alfombras |
| **cartridge** | filtro |
| **casing (window and door)** | marco |
| **caster** | rueda pivotante (loca), rueda de andamio rodante o movible |
| **catastrophe** | catástrofe [ka-TAS-tro-fe] |
| **catch** | gancho |
| **catch platform** | plataforma de detención |
| **caulking** | calafateo |
| **ceiling** | techo |
| **ceiling beam** | viga del plafón, viga de techo |
| **ceiling box** | caja de techo |
| **ceiling fixture** | ornamento de techo |
| **ceiling value** | valor máximo |
| **cement** | cemento |
| **cement mixer** | hormigonera |
| **center** | centro |
| **central hub** | collarín |

| | |
|---|---|
| **chainsaw** | moto-sierra |
| **chain sprocket** | rueda dentada de cadena, cadena montada |
| **chair rail molding** | moldura de sillas |
| **chalk** | tiza |
| **chalkline** | cordón de tiza |
| **chamber** | cámara |
| **change rooms** | habitaciones para vestirse |
| **check** | cheque |
| **check list** | lista de cotejo, lista de control |
| **chemicals** | químicos |
| **chest illness** | enfermedad pulmonar |
| **chest roentgenogram** | radiografía del pecho |
| **chicken ladder** | tablón con listones |
| **chimney** | chimenea |
| **chipper** | astilladora |
| **chipper spout** | tubo de descarga de la astilladora |
| **chipping operation** | operación de picar |
| **chisel** | cincel, escoplo |
| **chute** | conducto |
| **circuit** | circuito |
| **circuit tester** | probador de circuitos |
| **circular** | sierra circular |
| **citation** | citación [si-ta-SYON] |

| | |
|---|---|
| **city main** | acueducto |
| **clam caps** | casquillos de grampas |
| **clamp** | abrazadera |
| **claw** | chivo |
| **claw hammer** | martillo chivo |
| **cleanout** | registro |
| **clear** | espacio libre |
| **clearance** | espacio |
| **clip-on bracket** | palometa de presión |
| **closed cup (flash point)** | copa cerrada (punto de inflamación) |
| **closure valves** | válvulas de cierre |
| **cloth** | trapo |
| **clutch** | embrague |
| **coal** | carbón de piedra |
| **coal for pitch** | brea de alquitrán de hulla |
| **coal naptha** | nafta de hulla |
| **coat (layer)** | capa |
| **coating** | revestimiento |
| **code** | código |
| **coiled welding cable** | cable de soldar en espiral |
| **cold-formed heads** | cabezales formados en frío |
| **color** | color |
| **column** | columna |
| **combs** | peines |
| **combustion air inlet** | toma de aire para combustión |
| **compactor** | compactador |

| | |
|---|---|
| **company** | compañía [kam-pan-YI-a], empresa [em-PRE-sa] |
| **complainant** | querellante [ke-re-YAN-te], quejista [ke-HIS-ta], demandante [de-man-DAN-te], denunciante [de-nun-SYAN-te], reclamante [re-kla-MAN-te] |
| **complaint** | queja [KE-ha], querella [ke-RE-ya], demanda [de-MAN-da], denuncia [de-NUN-sya], reclamo [re-KLA-mo] |
| **compliance assistance** | asistencia en cumplimiento [a-sis-TEN-sya en cum-pli-MYEN-to], asistencia para conformidad [a-sis-TEN-sya PA-ra kon-for-mi-DAD] |
| **comply** | cumplir [kum-PLIR] |
| **compressor** | compresor |
| **compressor cutoff** | cierre para el compresor |

| | |
|---|---|
| concrete | concreto |
| concrete board | tabla de concreto |
| concrete breaker | martillo rompe-concreto |
| concrete pad | plataforma de hormigón, de concreto |
| concrete vibrators | vibrador para hormigón, para concreto |
| condenser | condensador |
| conduit (metal) | conducto de metal |
| conduit (PVC) | conducto de PVC |
| cone-pulley belt | correa de polea (escalonada) |
| cones | conos |
| confining wall | pared circundante |
| connecting rod | varilla, barra, vara (de conexión) |
| connector, crimp | conector de alambre aplastado |
| continuous bleaching range | instalación de blanqueo continuo |
| continuous flow type (flow mode) | tipo de flujo continuo |
| contour gauge | indicador de contornos |
| control circuit | circuito de mando |
| controller cabinets | cabina de mando |
| contruction | construcción |
| conveyor | transportador |
| cooker | cocedor para |

| | |
|---|---|
| | encolar, cocedor |
| **copper** | cobre |
| **cordeau detonant fuse** | cuerda detonante |
| **core collar** | collar central |
| **core shaft** | eje central |
| **corner (inside)** | rincón |
| **corner (outside)** | esquina |
| **corner bead** | protector de esquinas |
| **cotter pin** | pasador de chaveta |
| **cotton blend** | mezcla de algodón |
| **cotton combers** | peinadora para algodón |
| **cotton dust** | polvo de algodón |
| **cotton waste** | borra de algodón |
| **counterblow equipment** | equipo de contragolpe |
| **countersunk** | avellanado |
| **coupler block** | bloque de unión |
| **coupling** | copla |
| **course** | curso |
| **cover** | cubierta |
| **coveralls** | mono |
| **coverings (head, foot)** | protección para la cabeza, protección para los pies |
| **crack (glass, porcelain)** | raja |
| **crack (wood,wall)** | grieta |
| **crank arm** | biela |
| **crashrail** | baranda para colisión |
| **cratering** | abolladura |

| | |
|---|---|
| **crawler locomotive** | locomotora de oruga |
| **cross beam** | viga transversal |
| **cross brace** | cruceta, refuerzo transversal |
| **cross bracing** | reforzamiento transversal |
| **cross head** | cabezal |
| **cross role brakes** | amasadores de rodillo cruzado |
| **cross ventilation** | ventilación cruzada |
| **cross-grain** | grano transversal |
| **crowbar** | palanca |
| **crown face** | cara combada |
| **crown molding** | moldura para la cornisa |
| **crown wheel** | rueda central |
| **cryogenic temperatures** | temperaturas criogénicas |
| **culvert** | alcantarilla |
| **cupback bushing** | casquillo acopado |
| **curb** | Bordillo |
| **cut-off point** | punto de corte final, parada final |
| **cylinder shaker** | agitador de cilindro |
| **cytotoxic** | cito- tóxico |
| **danger** | peligro |
| **dangerous** | peligroso |
| **dead air pocket** | bolsillo de aire viciado |
| **dead front receptacles** | receptáculos de frente muerto |

| | |
|---|---|
| dead-weight test | prueba de carga completa |
| debris | escombro |
| decision making circuitry | circuito de decisión |
| deck (outside) | terraza |
| deck (subfloor) | loso de desplante |
| decorator scaffold | andamio para decorador |
| deep seated condition | condiciones críticas |
| deluge showers | duchas de seguridad de lluvia artificial intensa |
| deluge system | sistema de inundación |
| demonstrate | demostrar |
| department | departamento |
| deposition | deposición |
| depth gauge | medidor de profundidad |
| derail block | calzado para descarrilamiento |
| design | diseño |
| detent | retén |
| detonating primers | cartuchos detonantes |
| develop | desarrollar |
| diagonal bracing | abrazadera diagonal |
| diagonal cutter | cortadora de diagonales |
| die (power presses) | troquel |
| die casting | fundición en troquel |

| | |
|---|---|
| **steoreotyping** | para estereotipo |
| **diesel fuel** | combustible diesel |
| **digging bar** | palanca excavadora |
| **digital multimeter** | milímetro digital |
| **digs** | perforaciones |
| **dimmer** | regulador de luz |
| **director** | director |
| **dirt** | tierra |
| **discharge stack** | pabellón de descarga |
| **disciplinary** | disciplinario |
| **discipline** | disciplina |
| **disconnecting means** | manera de desconectar, forma de desconectar, mecanismo de desconectar |
| **discrimination** | discrimen, discriminación |
| **disease** | enfermedad |
| **dispensing device** | aparatos de suministro |
| **display** | exhibir, mostrar |
| **ditch** | zanja |
| **division** | división |
| **doctor blades** | cuchilla raspadora |
| **document** | documento |
| **dolly** | plataforma rodante |
| **eoor** | Puerta |
| **double** | doble |
| **double cleat ladder** | escalera doble de listones |

| | |
|---|---|
| **downstream** | corriente descendente |
| **drag brake** | freno para decelerar |
| **drain** | de desagüe |
| **drainboard** | drenaje |
| **draw** | estirar |
| **drawing frame** | máquina de estirado |
| **drift point** | punto de desplazamiento |
| **drip pan** | bandeja recoge-gotas |
| **drive roll** | rodillo accionado |
| **driving flange** | pestaña guía |
| **drop forged steel** | acero forjado |
| **drop hammer** | martillo de forja |
| **dry chemical** | substancia química en polvo, químico en polvo |
| **dry gas meter** | medidor de gas seco |
| **dry standpipe system** | sistema de columna de alimentación de agua; vacío |
| **dry type overspray collectors** | recolector del exceso de rocío seco |
| **drying can** | tambor secador |
| **dual component coating** | revestimiento con dos elementos |
| **duct velocity** | velocidad en el conducto |
| **dumbwaiter** | montacargas |
| **dust collection** | recolectores de |

| | |
|---|---|
| | polvo |
| **dust respirator** | respirador para polvo, respirador mecánico para polvo |
| **duster** | bayeta |
| **egress** | salida, medios de salida |
| **elbow** | codo |
| **electric blasting cap** | detonador eléctrico |
| **electric runway conductor** | sistema de conductor eléctrico |
| **electric safety flashlight** | linterna de batería |
| **electric safety lantern** | linterna eléctrica |
| **electrode lead cable** | cable conductor de electrodo |
| **electrostatic atomizing head** | atomizadores electrostáticos |
| **elevating work platform** | plataforma de trabajo elevadiza, plataforma para trabajo a varios niveles |
| **embosser** | estampar en relieve |
| **emergency disposal** | vaciado de emergencia |
| **employee (s)** | trabajador(es) [tra-ba-DOR / tra-ba-DOR-es], empleado(s) [em-ple-A-do(s), obrero(s) [o-BRE- |

| | |
|---|---|
| | ro(s)] |
| **employee representative** | representante de los trabajadores / empleados [re-pre-sen-TAN-te de los tr-ba-DOR-es / em-ple-A-dos] |
| **employer** | representante del empleador [re-pre-sen-TAN-te del em-ple-A-dor], patrono [pat-RO-no], patrón [pat-RON], jefe [HE-fe], empresario [em-pre-SAR-yo] |
| **enclosing hood** | campana de cubierta |
| **enclosing screen** | malla protectora |
| **enclosure** | encerramiento, protector cerrado |
| **end** | del extremo |
| **enforce** | imponer [im-po-NER |
| **engine drum extractor** | tambor exprimidor motorizado |
| **erythema** | eritema |
| **establishment** | establecimiento [es-tab-le-si-MYEN-to] |
| **evaporation rate** | promedio de evaporación, razón de evaporación, tasa de evaporación |

| | |
|---|---|
| **excelsior** | viruta; paja de madera |
| **exhaust** | de extracción |
| **exhaust slot** | ranura de extracción |
| **exhaust ventilation** | ventilación para extracción |
| **exit** | Salida |
| **exit access** | acceso a la salida |
| **exit discharge** | salida de descarga, salida final |
| **exit stairs** | escaleras de escape, de salida |
| **explosion actuated fastening tool** | herramientas para sujetar accionadas por explosivos |
| **explosion venting** | escape de explosión |
| **explosion venting areas** | escape de explosión |
| **extension light** | lámpara con extensión |
| **extension platform** | plataforma de extensión |
| **exterior** | Exterior |
| **extrusions** | extrusión, estirado a presión |
| **eye flushes** | fuente para lavado de ojos |
| **face shield** | mascara |
| **face-piece-to-face seal** | que la máscara selle la cara |
| **fail-safe control** | control automático de protección |
| **fall arrester** | sistema de |

| | detención de caídas |
|---|---|
| **falling objects** | caída de objetos, objetos volantes |
| **false bottom** | fondo doble |
| **false floor** | piso falso |
| **fan** | ventilador |
| **fastener driver** | impulsor de fijadores |
| **faucet** | llave de agua |
| **felt** | felpa |
| **fence** | cerca |
| **ferrule** | casquillo |
| **fertilizer** | fertilizante |
| **fiberglass** | fibra de vidrio |
| **fiberglass box guide** | indicador en caja de fibra de vidrio |
| **field monitor cassette** | porta-filtro para la toma de muestra en el campo |
| **file** | lima |
| **fill spout** | boquilla de llenado |
| **fill stem** | tubo de llenado |
| **filler block** | bloque de relleno |
| **filler holder** | soporte del filtro |
| **filler metal** | metal de aportación |
| **filler strip** | listón de relleno |
| **filling pipe inlet terminal** | terminal de la tubería de llenado |
| **film badge** | dosímetro fotográfico personal |
| **film ring** | dosímetro anular |
| **filter** | filtro |

| | |
|---|---|
| **final terminal stopping device** | mecanismo auxiliar de detención final |
| **fines** | polvos |
| **finish (of a surface)** | acabado |
| **fire aisles** | pasillos de salida, pasadizos de escape |
| **fire door** | puerta a prueba de fuego, puerta ignífuga |
| **fire resistance rating** | tasa de resistencia al fuego |
| **fireplace** | chimenea |
| **first aid** | primeros auxilios |
| **fish tape** | cinta pescadora |
| **fitting** | accesorio, conector |
| **fitting-Y** | en Y (ee-gree-ay-gah) |
| **fittting-T** | en T (tay) |
| **fixed ladder** | escalera fija, escala fija |
| **flagman** | abanderado |
| **flammable vapor-air mixtures** | mezclas inflamables de vapor con aire |
| **flange** | platillo, pestañas, brida |
| **flange facings** | revestimiento de las pestañas |
| **flanged** | de brida, reborde, pestaña |
| **flash arrester** | pararrayos |
| **flashing** | tapajuntas |
| **flashlight** | linterna |

| | |
|---|---|
| **flashpoint** | punto de llama, punto de inflamación |
| **flat work ironers** | prensa de planchar |
| **float scaffold** | andamio colgante |
| **floating roof** | techo flotante |
| **floats** | base de los estabilizadores |
| **floodlight** | reflector de haz difuso |
| **floor** | piso, suelo |
| **floor stand machine** | máquina con soporte de piso |
| **flooring** | piso |
| **flooring strips** | tiras |
| **flourescente** | fluorescente |
| **flow rate** | tasa de flujo, razón de flujo, medida del caudal |
| **fluidized bed** | lecho fluidificado |
| **flux** | fundir (sobre soldadura), flujo |
| **flux** | fundente |
| **folding** | plegadiza |
| **follow-up inspections** | inspección de verificación [in-spek-SYON de ve-ri-fi-CA-syon], inspección de seguimiento [in-spek-SYON de se-gi-MYEN-to] |

| | |
|---|---|
| **foot ladder board** | tabla de seguridad para apoyo |
| **foot walk** | andén |
| **footing** | base de apoyo |
| **footing** | zarpa, cimiento |
| **forced vital capacity** | capacidad vital (FVC) |
| **fork truck** | montacargas, carretilla de horquilla |
| **forklift** | montacargas |
| **form scaffold** | andamio de molde |
| **forming** | modelado, conformar |
| **forms** | encofrados |
| **foundation** | cimiento |
| **framing** | armadura, marco |
| **free standing mobile scaffold tower** | torre de andamio movible independiente |
| **freely suspended load** | carga suspendida libremente, carga de suspensión libre |
| **fringe** | ribete, borde |
| **front** | parte delantera |
| **front-end loader** | cargador delantero |
| **fuel** | combustible |
| **fuel gas outlet** | tubo de descarga para gas |
| **fulcrum point** | punto de apoyo |
| **full facepiece powered air purifying respirator** | máscara purificadora de aire |

| | |
|---|---|
| | motorizada |
| **full facepiece with:** | máscara completa con: |
| **full hydrostatic head** | presión hidrostática completa, cabezal hidrostático completo |
| **full trailer van** | remolque |
| **furnace** | calentador |
| **furnace** | calentador |
| **fuse disconnect switch** | interrumpir con fusible, disyuntor con fusible |
| **fuse igniter** | encendedor de mecha |
| **fuse lighters** | fusible de encendido |
| **fused** | fusión |
| | |
| **gable roof** | techo inclinado |
| **gaff** | trepadores para postes, dientes |
| **galvanizing tank** | tanque de galvanización |
| **gambrel roof** | techo abuhardillado |
| **gang sam** | sierra múltiple |
| **gantry crane** | grúa de pórtico |
| **gap** | espacio |
| **garage** | del garaje |
| **garbage disposer** | triturador |
| **garnetting** | desfibrado de algodón, deshilado |

| | |
|---|---|
| | de algodón |
| **gas (for heating)** | gas |
| **gas (for vehicle)** | gasolina |
| **gas bell** | campana de gas |
| **gas chromatography** | cromatografía de gas |
| **gas holder** | depósito de gas |
| **gas line** | línea de gas |
| **gas mask, front or back mounted canister** | máscara antigás con cartucho colocado en el pecho o sobre la espalda |
| **gaskets and thread sealants** | arandelas/selladores de juntas |
| **gasoline** | gasolina [gas-o-LI-na] |
| **gasometer principle** | principio de gasómetro |
| **gas-shielded arc welding** | soldadura por arco protegido por gas inerte |
| **gauge** | indicador |
| **generator, backup** | generador de emergencia |
| **gin pole** | mástil-guía |
| **girder** | viga principal |
| **gloves** | guantes |
| **glue** | pegamento, goma |
| **goggles** | lentes de seguridad |
| **gouges** | hendiduras |
| **governor tripping speed** | velocidad de disparo del |

| | |
|---|---|
| | regulador, velocidad de desembrague del regulador |
| **grab rail** | barra de agarre |
| **grab samples** | muestras al azar |
| **grader** | criba separadora |
| **grading** | gradación, preparaci6n del terreno |
| **gravel** | grava |
| **gravity head** | presión por gravedad |
| **gray cast iron** | hierro de fundición gris |
| **grid** | sistema de rejas |
| **grid guard** | resguardo de rejilla |
| **grinder** | esmeriladora, pulidora, afiladora, trituradora |
| **grinding** | raspado |
| **ground-fault circuit interrupter (GFCI)** | interruptor de circuito con pérdida a tierra [in-ter-rup-TOR de sir-KI-to kon PER-di-da a TYER-ra] , interruptor a tierra / fallo [in-ter-rup-TOR a TYER-ra / FA-yo] |
| **grout** | lechada, relleno, |

| | |
|---|---|
| | mezcla de cemento |
| **grout** | lechada |
| **grout float** | flota de calidad |
| **guard** | guarda [WAR-da], resguardo [res-WAR-do] |
| **guardrail** | baranda |
| **guardrail system** | sistema de barandas [sis-TE-ma de bar-AN-das] |
| **gudgeon** | pasador de eje |
| **guide (for door)** | guía |
| **guide post** | poste-guía |
| **guide roller** | rodillo-guía |
| **guide shoe** | zapata de guía |
| **guideline** | línea de guía |
| **gutter** | canaleta, canalón |
| **guy (brace, guide)** | cuerda, soga, cable, soguería |
| **guy derrick** | cabria rotativa de vientos |
| | |
| **hacksaw** | sierra con marco, serrucho para metal |
| **hammer** | martillo |
| **hammer operated piston tool** | herramienta de émbolo/pistón accionada por martillo |
| **hammer tacker (stapler)** | grapadora martillo |
| **hammer test** | prueba con martillo |

| | |
|---|---|
| handsaw | serrucho |
| hand bailing machine | rebobinadora manual |
| hand line | cuerdas de mano |
| hand steering wheel | guía manual, timón manual |
| hand-fed crosscut table saw | sierra de tronzar de alimentación manual y de mesa |
| handrail | pasamano, baranda |
| handsaw | sierra de mano |
| hanger | gancho |
| hanger (pipe) | gancho para tubos |
| hard deep-cutting abrasives | abrasivo fuerte |
| hard hat | casco |
| hardwood | madera dura |
| hatchway | escotilla |
| hawk (drywall) | llana enyesadura |
| hazard (s) | riesgo(s) [ri-ES-go(s)], peligro(s) [pe-LI-gro(s)] |
| hazard communication | comunicación de riesgos [ko-mu-ni-ka-SYON de ri-ES-gos] |
| head pulley shaft | eje de la polea matriz |
| head rig | instalación principal |
| head saw | sierra maestra |
| head stock | cabezal |
| headband | cinta de ajuste para |

| | |
|---|---|
| | la cabeza |
| **header** | cabezal |
| **headroom** | espacio superior, espacio adecuado, margen de altura mínima |
| **health hazard** | Riesgo contra la salud [ri-ES-go KON-tra la sal-UD], peligro a la salud [pe-LI-gro a la sal-UD] |
| **hearing loss** | perdida de audición [per-DI-da de auw-di-SYON] |
| **heat exchanger** | repartidor de calefacción |
| **heater** | calderas, calentador |
| **heater, hot-water** | calentador del agua |
| **heating** | calefacción |
| **heavy equipment** | equipo pesado |
| **heavy mass hammer** | martillo macizo |
| **heavy timber** | madero pesado |
| **helmet** | casco [KAS-ko] |
| **hematopoietic system** | sistema de formación de la sangre |
| **hemoglobinopthies** | hemoglobinopatías |
| **Hg** | mercurio |
| **high efficiency filter respirator** | máscara completa con filtro de gran |

| | |
|---|---|
| | eficacia |
| **high energy rate forming machine** | prensas de forjar de platos accionados por gas comprimido |
| **high explosives** | explosivos instantáneos |
| **high lift rider truck** | carretilla elevadora de gran alcance |
| **high-energy-rate** | energía a gran velocidad |
| **high-voltage grid** | parrilla de alta tensión |
| **highway** | autopista, carretera |
| **hinge** | bisagra |
| **hitch (car,truck)** | llevar |
| **hitch (to)** | acoplar |
| **hoe** | azadón |
| **hoisting drum** | tambor elevado, tambor para levantar, elevar |
| **hoisting tackle (chain)** | cabrestante de cadena |
| **hold-down** | pieza de anclaje |
| **holddown roll** | rodillo de sujeción |
| **hole (in ground)** | hueco [WE-ko] |
| **hole (small)** | hoyo |
| **hole (small)** | agujero |
| **hollow pan type thread** | huella acanalada |
| **hook** | gancho |
| **hook-over bracket** | soporte, escala de gancho, palometa de gancho |

| | |
|---|---|
| hooper | tolva |
| horizontal channel | canales horizontales |
| horizontal dough mixer | batidora horizontal |
| horse scaffold | andamio de caballete, andamio de burros |
| hose | manguera |
| hose rack | portamangueras |
| hot-formed heads | cabezales formados al calor |
| hot-water heater | calentador del agua |
| hot-water radiant heating | calefacción por inducción de agua caliente |
| hour | hora |
| hourly rating | rendimiento por hora |
| house wrap (water & wind resistant) | envoltura de material resistente al agua y al viento |
| houses | casas |
| housing | recinto, caja |
| housing member | pieza de encaje |
| hub | collarín |
| HVAC | calefacción, ventilación y aire acondicionado |
| hygiene | higiene [I-jyen] |
| I- beam | vigas doble T |
| igniters | encendedores |

|  |  |
|---|---|
| **illness (es)** | enfermedad (es) [en-fer-me-DAD / en-fer-me-DAD-es] |
| **imminent danger** | peligro inminente [pe-LI-gro in-mi-NEN-te] |
| **impact noise** | ruido por impacto |
| **impounding basin** | embalse, área de retención |
| **impulsive noise** | ruido interrumpido |
| **inch** | pulgada [pul-GA-da] |
| **inclined egress components** | medios de salida inclinados |
| **income** | ingresos |
| **indented mullions** | montantes oprimidos |
| **independent pole scaffold** | andamio de poste de madera independiente |
| **individual** | individual |
| **individual shackle rod** | varillaje de sujeción individual |
| **industrial hygiene(ist)** | higiene (higienista) |
| **inhalation** | inhalar [in-al-AR], aspirar [as-pir-AR] |
| **initiating device** | dispositivo de accionamiento |
| **injury (ies)** | lesión (es) [le-SYON / le-SYON-es] |
| **in-running roll** | rodillo alimentador |

| | |
|---|---|
| **inspect** | inspeccionar [in-spek-syon-AR] |
| **instructions** | instrucciones |
| **insulation** | aislamiento [ais-la-MYEN-to] |
| **interior hung scaffold** | andamio colgante para interiores |
| **interlocking circuitry** | circuito de cierre |
| **intersecting faller** | peines de entrecruce |
| **intervening room spaces** | espacios intermedios entre habitaciones |
| **interview** | entrevista [en-tre-VIS-ta] |
| **investigation** | investigación [in-ves-ti-ga-SYON] |
| **inward air velocity** | velocidad del aire centripeto |
| **isolated right bundle branch block** | bloque de rama derecha (aislado) |
| **J- box** | cámara en J |
| | |
| **jack (lifter)** | gato |
| **jack (trimmer)** | montante para sostener el cabezal |
| **jack hammer** | martillo neumático |
| **jack ladder** | escala de gato; rampa de entrada (aserraderos) |
| **jack scaffold** | andamio de palometa, andamio de escala |

| | |
|---|---|
| **jacket (mixer)** | camisa exterior |
| **jig saw** | sierra coladora |
| **job** | trabajo |
| **jog** | avance lento |
| **joint** | junta |
| **joint compound** | compuesto de juntas |
| **joint tape** | cinta para juntas |
| **jointer** | cepillo mecánico |
| **joist** | viga, vigueta |
| **joist hanger** | estribos para viguetas |
| **jumper cables** | cables de arranque |
| **junctions** | confluencias |
| **jurisdiction** | jurisdicción [hu-ris-dik-SYON |
| | |
| **kegs** | barril |
| **key** | llave |
| **key** | acoplar, cuñas para martillo |
| **kiln** | secador |
| **knee brace** | esquinal |
| **knee pads** | protector de rodillas |
| **knife** | cuchillo |
| **knife head of reciprocating blade slicers** | rebanadoras de cuchilla de vaivén |
| **knowledge** | conocimiento [ko-no-si-MYEN-to] |
| | |
| **label** | etiqueta [e-ti-KE-ta] |
| **ladder** | escalera |

| | |
|---|---|
| **ladder (portable)** | escalera portátil [es-ka-LE-ra] |
| **ladder -10'** | -de diez pies |
| **ladder -16'** | -de dieciséis pies |
| **Ladder -24'** | -de veinticuatro pies |
| **ladder -28'** | -de veintiocho pies |
| **ladder -32'** | -de treinta y dos pies |
| **ladder -40'** | -de cuarenta pies |
| **ladder -6'** | -de seis pies |
| **ladder jack scaffold** | andamio de palometas en escalera |
| **ladder-type platform** | plataforma tipo escalera |
| **laminate** | de laminado |
| **landing** | descanso |
| **landing platform** | plataforma de descanso |
| **lanyard** | cuerda de seguridad [KWER-da de se-gu-ri-DAD], cordón [kor-DON], pila [PI-la] |
| **large area scaffold** | andamio de área grande |
| **large bubble meter** | medidor con bureta |
| **last name** | apellido [a-pe-YI-do] |
| **law** | ley |
| **layout** | trazo |
| **lead (fuel)** | fuga (de |

| | |
|---|---|
| | combustible) |
| lead | plomo |
| leak (pipe) | gotera |
| lean to scaffold | andamio reclinado |
| leg (scaffold) | pata (andamio) |
| leg irons | hierros curvos |
| leukopenia | leucopenia |
| level egress components | medios de salida a nivel |
| lid | tapa |
| life jacket | chaleco salvavidas [cha-LE-ko sal-va-VI-das] |
| lifeline | cuerda de seguridad [KWER-da de se-gu-ri-DAD] |
| lift truck | montacargas para elevar, carretilla elevadora |
| lifter roof | techo levadizo |
| light fixture | lámpara, luz |
| light,flood | reflector de haz difuso |
| light-field techniques | microscopio corriente |
| limit switch | interruptor de seguridad |
| limiting value | valor límite |
| line | línea |
| linear actuators | impulsor de línea |
| linoleum | linóleo |
| lint-free respirable | polvo de algodón |

| | |
|---|---|
| **cotton dust** | respirable sin borra |
| **liquified petroleum gas** | gas licuado de petróleo |
| **live roll** | rodillo activo |
| **load back rest extension** | prolongación del respaldo contra carga |
| **load black** | cuadernal desplazable |
| **load engaging means** | mecanismo para engranaje de la carga |
| **loaded stream** | chorro de agua |
| **loading boom** | vara para cargar |
| **locked out** | fijar en posición de abierto |
| **locking device** | dispositivo inmovilizador |
| **lockout** | interrupción de energía usando candado, cierre de corriente, disyuntor |
| **lockout/tagout** | interrupción de energía usando candado y etiqueta [in-ter-rup-SYON de en-er-HI-a us-AN-do kan-DA-do i e-ti-KE-ta] |
| **lockset** | cerradura |
| **lofts** | galerías |
| **loom fixer** | persona encargada |

| | |
|---|---|
| | de fijar el telar |
| **Lot** | parcela |
| **low temperature shutoff switch** | interruptor para corte a baja temperatura, interruptor de cierre a baja temperatura |
| **lugs** | uñas, anillos |
| **luterman** | sellador de horno |
| | |
| **machine (n)** | máquina [MA-ki-na] |
| **machine operator, coke side** | operador de máquina del lado del coque |
| **magnetic controller** | mando magnético |
| **makeup air** | aire limpio |
| **mallet** | mazo |
| **management** | |
| **management** | administración [ad-min-is-tra-SYON], gerencia[he-REN-sya], manejo [Man-EY-ho] |
| **mandatory** | obligatorio |
| **maneuver** | método |
| **manhole** | registro [re-HE-stro], pozo de registro |
| **manlift** | elevadores para personal, elevadores |

| | para trabajadores |
|---|---|
| **manual input** | elemento de alimentación manual |
| **manual reset** | reprogramación manual |
| **manually operated winches** | malacates operados manualmente |
| **mark service pressure** | presión establecida de servicio |
| **masking tape** | cinta adhesiva protectora |
| **masonry** | albañilería [al-ban-yi-le-RI-a] |
| **masonry material** | material de albañilería |
| **mason's adjustable multiple-point suspension scaffold** | andamio ajustable de suspensión múltiple (para albañiles) |
| **material (substance)** | material |
| **mattock** | zapapico |
| **maximal inspiration volume** | volumen de inspiración máxima |
| **maximum intended load** | carga máxima designada |
| **maximum peak** | valor máximo |
| **maximum spring deflection** | desviación máxima del muelle |
| **means of egress** | modo de salida [MO-do de sa-LI-da] |

| | |
|---|---|
| measurements | medidas |
| measuring tape | cinta para medir [SIN-ta PA-ra ME-dir], cinta metro [SIN-ta ME-tro] |
| mechanical irritants | irritantes industriales |
| mechanical power-press | prensa mecánica automática |
| mechanical power-transmission guard | resguardo mecánico, guarda para transmisión de energía |
| mechanical stop | inmovilizador mecánico |
| mechanical ventilation | ventilación mecánica, presión mecánica impelente |
| mercerizing range | instalación de mercerización |
| metal | metal |
| metal angle | angular de metal |
| metal bracket form scaffold | andamio de molde con palometa de metal |
| metal combs | colectores metálicos |
| metal horns | boquilla metálica |
| metal plate | plancha de metal |
| meter | metro [ME-tro] |
| middle rail (scaffold) | larguero intermedio (andamio), baranda del medio, madero |

| | |
|---|---|
| | intermedio |
| **midget bubbler** | bureta pequeña |
| **midrail** | larguero intermedio, baranda del medio, madero intermedio |
| **mid-season retest** | re-examen de mediados de temporada |
| **mild loading** | carga contraviento |
| **mild steel** | acero dúctil |
| **mildew** | moho [MO-oh] |
| **mills** | fresadoras, torno (metal) |
| **minimum crushing strength** | resistencia mínima a la compresión |
| **minimum road clearance** | margen de altura mínima desde el chasis hasta la carretera |
| **misfires** | mechazos, tiros fallados |
| **mistakes** | errores |
| **miter** | |
| **miter box** | caja de ángulos |
| **miter saw** | sierra ingletadora, sierra de retroceso para ingletes |
| **mobile** | sobre ruedas, a móvil |
| **mobile supply trucks** | camiones móviles de abastecimiento |

| | |
|---|---|
| mode selection element | elemento para la selección de graduación |
| molding | moldura |
| money | dinero |
| monitoring | programa de detección |
| mortar | mortero, mezcla |
| motor | motor |
| motor controller | regulador del motor |
| motor couplings | uniones del motor |
| motor vehicle | vehículo de motor [ve-I-ku-lo de MO-tor] |
| motor vehicle cargo tank | camión tanque |
| motor vehicle cargo tanks | tanques de carga motorizados; camión tanque |
| moving stairways | escalera mecánica |
| mud sill (on scaffold) | madero colocado en las patas de los andamios para darles apoyo o sostén |
| muffler | silenciador |
| nail pouch | bolsa para los clavos |
| nailgun | clavadora neumática |
| nailgun, flooring | clavadora |
| nailgun, framing | neumática para |

| | |
|---|---|
| **nailgun, roofing** | pisos |
| **nailgun, trim/finish** | clavadora de armazón |
| | clavadora neumática para techar |
| | clavadora para el acabado |
| **needle beam** | viga de espiga |
| **needle beam scaffold** | andamio de espiga, andamio de parihuela |
| **nibbler** | recortadora de chapa |
| **noise** | ruido [Roo-EE-dough] |
| **non deposited air-suspended powder** | polvo no depositado y suspendido en el aire |
| **non drums end of the hoisting ropes** | los extremos de los cables de izar que no se enrollan en tambores |
| **non textile workers** | trabajadores en empleos no textiles |
| **nonkick back dogs** | grapas contra-rechazador |
| **nonkick back fingers** | uñas contra-rechazador |
| **notcher** | entallador |
| **nuts** | tuercas |
| **occupancies** | espacios ocupados |

| | |
|---|---|
| **occupant load** | cabida |
| **occupational** | ocupacional [o-ku-pa-SYON-al], laboral [la-bor-AL], en el trabajo [en el tra-BA-ho] |
| **oil** | aceite |
| **oil free (air, nitrogen, carbon dioxide)** | sin residuos de petróleo (aire, nitrógeno, dióxido de carbono) |
| **open-circuit** | circuito abierto |
| **open circuit self-contained breathing apparatus** | equipo de respiración auto contenido de circuito abierto |
| **open circuit self-contained breathing apparatus** | equipo de respiración de circuito abierto auto-contenido |
| **open cup tester** | tomadores de prueba de copa abierta |
| **open end hollow rung** | peldaño hueco de extremo abierto |
| **open fat kettles** | calderas abiertas para freír con grasa |
| **open floor area** | área al descubierto |
| **open frame hammer** | martillo de forja de armazón abierto |
| **open space** | espacio abierto |
| **open wave guide** | guía de onda abierta |

| | |
|---|---|
| open wire | circuito abierto |
| open-face filter holder | sujetador de filtro abierto |
| opening (in wall, etc.) | brecha |
| opening pressure | presión inicial |
| operating bus linkage | conexión de mando de la barra distribuidora |
| operating device | mecanismo de control |
| operating ropes | cables de maniobra, sogas de operación |
| organic vapor gas mask | máscara para vapores orgánicos |
| outdoor | de afuera |
| outlet | receptáculo [re-sep-TA-ku-lo] |
| outlet covers (wall plates) | cubiertos de enchufes, Placas de pared |
| outlet, 120v | enchufe de 120 (ciento veinte) voltios |
| outlet, 240v | enchufe de 240 (doscientos cuarenta) voltios |
| output element | elemento de extracción |
| outrigger beam | viga voladiza, viga saliente o que sobresale |

| | |
|---|---|
| **outrigger ledger** | puente voladizo, madero saliente |
| **outrigger scaffold** | andamio voladizo |
| **outriggers** | estabilizadores |
| **overhead canopy hood** | campana de techo |
| **overhead crane** | grúa puente |
| **overhead governor** | control para alta velocidad |
| **overhead guard** | resguardo superior |
| **overshoes** | cubre-zapatos |
| **overspray** | exceso de rocío |
| **owner** | dueño [DWEN-yo] |
| **oxygen** | oxígeno [ok-SI-he-no] |
| **oxygen deficient** | deficiente en oxígeno [de-fi-SEN-te de ok-SI-he-no], nivel bajo de oxígeno [ni-VEL BA-ho de ok-SI-he-no] |
| **p.p.m.-parts of vapor or gas per million parts of contaminated air by volume at 25°C and 760 mm Hg pressure** | partes de vapor o gas por cada millón de partes de aire contaminado por volumen a 25°C y 760 mm de presión Hg (mercurio) |
| **packing or storage aids** | equipo para empaque o |

| | almacenaje |
|---|---|
| **padders** | almohadillas |
| **paddler** | paleta |
| **padlock** | disyuntor con candado, candado |
| **paint** | pintura |
| **paint remover** | removedor de pintura |
| **paint shield** | protector de pintura |
| **paint thinner** | diluyente de pintura |
| **pane (window)** | cristal, hoja, vidrio marcado |
| **panel** | panel |
| **panel raiser** | máquina de labrar paneles |
| **PAPR** | respirador purificador de aire forzado |
| **parquet** | parquet (tarima de madera ensamblada) |
| **part** | parte |
| **partition** | partición |
| **path of travel** | corredores |
| **pattern template** | patrón |
| **paver** | losa |
| **peak sound pressure level** | nivel máximo de la presión de sonido |
| **peanut cooling truck** | carro para enfriar maní |
| **peavys** | palanca de gancho |
| **penalize** | multar [mul-TAR] |

| | |
|---|---|
| penalty | multa [MUL-ta] |
| pendant push button | conmutadores colgantes |
| penetration asphalt (300) | asfalto con penetración 300 |
| permit required | permiso requerido [per-MI-so re-ke-RI-do] |
| person | persona [per-SO-na] |
| personal protective equipment | equipo de protección personal [e-KI-po de pro-tek-SYON per-son-AL] |
| personal sampling pump | bomba personal para tomar muestra |
| phenyl hydrade | hidruro de fenilo |
| photographic flash powder | polvo relámpago |
| pick | pico |
| pickup (act of collecting) | recogida |
| pickup truck | camioneta |
| picture hooks | ganchos para cuadros |
| picture rail | moldura para los cuadros |
| piece | pedazo |
| pier height | altura sobre pilares de hormigón, altura del muelle |
| pile | pila |
| pilot light | piloto |

|  |  |
|---|---|
| **pinch point** | punto de enganche, de agarre |
| **pipe-joint compound** | compuesto para tubos |
| **pipes** | tubos, mangueras |
| **piping, tubing** | tubería, cañería |
| **place of employment / workplace** | planta de trabajo [PLAN-ta de tra-BA-ho], lugar de trabajo [lu-GAR de tra-BA-ho] |
| **plan (drawing)** | plano |
| **planer** | acepilladora, cepillo, lijadora |
| **plank** | tablón |
| **plasterer's scaffold** | andamio de yesero |
| **plateau** | plató, altiplanicie |
| **Platform** | plataforma [plat-FOR-ma] |
| **plenum** | pleno |
| **pliers** | alicates |
| **pliers (lineman's)** | alicates para cortar cables |
| **pliers (needle nose)** | tenazas |
| **plow steel** | acero de mayor resistencia |
| **plug (electrical socket)** | toma de corriente |
| **plug (male connector to electrical socket)** | clavija |
| **plug (sink)** | tapón |
| **plumb bob** | plomo |

| | |
|---|---|
| **plumbing** | plomería [plo-me-RI-ya] |
| **plunger (toilet)** | desatascador, sopapa |
| **plywood** | madera contrachapada, laminada |
| **pneumatic powered tool** | herramienta neumática |
| **pocket chamber** | cámara de ionización de bolsillo |
| **pocket dosimeter** | dosímetro de bolsillo |
| **point (14 point gothic)** | punto (punto gótico 14) |
| **point type** | punto tipográfico |
| **pole (scaffold)** | poste (andamio) |
| **pole climbers** | trepadoras |
| **pole hole** | hoyo para poste |
| **pole scaffold** | andamio de poste |
| **pole scaffold** | andamio de poste |
| **port** | orificio de salida |
| **portable drinking water dispensers** | envases portátiles para repartir agua |
| **portable electric tool** | herramienta eléctrica de mano |
| **portable outlet leaders** | colectores de alimentación |
| **portable tanks** | depósitos, tanques portátiles |
| **portable trench box** | caja portátil para |

| | |
|---|---|
| | zanja |
| **positive displacement pump** | bomba de desplazamiento positivo (bomba volumétrica) |
| **positive grounding device** | dispositivo para conectar a tierra |
| **positive mechanical device** | dispositivo mecánico eficaz |
| **positive mechanical ventilation** | presión mecánica impelente, ventilación mecánica |
| **post** | poste |
| **poster** | cartel |
| **posthole-digger** | excavadora de hoyos |
| **potholes** | baches |
| **powder** | materia pulverizada, polvo |
| **powder coating** | revestir con materia pulverizada |
| **powder coating dust** | polvos producidos al revestir con materia pulverizada |
| **power auger (ground)** | barrena terrena |
| **power pack** | fuente de energía |
| **power painting device (paint sprayer)** | herramienta eléctrica de pintura |
| **power shovel** | pala mecánica |
| **power transmission and distribution** | transmisión y distribución de |

| | |
|---|---|
| | energía |
| **powered air purifying respirator** | respirador con purificador de aire motorizado |
| **powered air puriying respirator with high efficiency particulate filter** | respirador con purificador de aire motorizado con filtro de gran eficacia para partículas |
| **powered industrial truck** | camión industrial [kam-YON in-dus-TRYAL] |
| **powerline** | línea eléctrica |
| **power-transmission** | transmisión mecánica |
| **pre action system** | aviso preliminar |
| **pre-cut** | cortado |
| **prefabricated** | pre-fabricado |
| **prefinished** | pre-acabado |
| **preformed** | pre-formado |
| **pre-hung door** | puerta pre-fabricada |
| **preplacement** | exámenes para ubicación |
| **press bed** | bancada |
| **press brakes** | dobladora de chapas |
| **pressure** | presión [pre-SYON] |
| **pressure demand** | demanda de presión |
| **pressure drop** | caída de presión |
| **pressure roll** | cilindro superior |
| **pressure vessel** | recipiente a presión |
| **pressure-setting** | tendencia a |

| | |
|---|---|
| **tendency** | asentamiento por presión |
| **pressurized (closed bell)** | a presión (campana cerrada) |
| **presumed asbestos containing material (PACM)** | material que se presume contiene asbesto |
| **primary standard** | estándar primario |
| **prime movers** | motores primarios |
| **primed cartridges (explosive)** | cartuchos con cebo |
| **primer (paint base)** | pintura base |
| **printer** | imprimador |
| **printing machine** | estampadora, impresora |
| **probe** | sonda |
| **process equipment** | equipo elaborador procesador |
| **process vessel** | recipiente de procesamiento |
| **project** | proyecto |
| **projecting key** | cuña saliente (chaveta) |
| **projection hazard** | objetos salientes |
| **prolongs anchor** | punto de sujeción |
| **proofer** | probadores |
| **propane** | propano [pro-PA-no] |
| **protective ground** | conexión a tierra para brindar protección |
| **protective helmet** | casco de seguridad |

| | |
|---|---|
| **protective systems** | sistemas de protección |
| **proximity warning device** | aparato de aviso de proximidad |
| **pruners** | cortador de ramas |
| **pry bar** | pata de cabra |
| **P-trap** | Sifón tipo P |
| **pulley** | polea |
| **pulling ring** | equipo de halar o jalar |
| **pulling tension** | tensión por tracción, tensión al halar o jalar |
| **pulp chips** | astillas para pasta papelera |
| **pulpwood** | madera para pasta papelera |
| **pump** | bomba |
| **pump jack bracket** | palometa de gato, escala de gato |
| **pump jack scaffold** | andamio de palometa de gato |
| **pump jack scaffold** | andamio de palometa de gato |
| **pumpcrete system** | sistema para bombeo de concreto |
| **punching** | punzadora |
| **putlog** | palo de almojaya |
| **putty** | masilla |
| **putty knife** | espátula |
| **PVC pipe** | tubería de plástico |

| | |
|---|---|
| **qualified person** | persona cualificada [per-SO-na kwa-li-fi-CA-da] |
| **quart** | cuarto |
| **quarter mask** | respirador que protege la nariz y la boca sin cubrir la barbilla |
| **quenching car operator** | operador de carro de templar |
| **question** | pregunta [pre-GOON-ta] |
| **R-20 insulation** | aislamiento de R veinte [ER-ray VAIN-tay] |
| **radiant heating coil** | serpentín para calefacción por inducción |
| **radiant floor heating** | calentamiento radiante de piso |
| **rafter** | viga, travesaño |
| **rag** | trapo |
| **rail clamps** | abrazadera de anclaje al carril |
| **rail tankcars** | vagones cisterna |
| **railing** | baranda |
| **railing (fence)** | reja |
| **rake** | rastrillo |
| **rake board** | moldura del techo |
| **ram** | pistón, émbolo |
| **random spray** | rociado de manera |

| | arbitraria |
|---|---|
| **rasp** | raspadora |
| **ratchet** | trinquete |
| **ratchet wrench** | llave de trinquete |
| **rated busting pressure** | presión de estallido calculada |
| **rated load** | carga calculada |
| **ready-mix truck** | camión de pre-mezclado, mezcla-lista |
| **rebar** | varilla, acero de refuerzo |
| **receptacle outlet** | receptáculo |
| **recess** | recoveco |
| **reciprocating components** | piezas oscilantes |
| **reciprocating saw** | sierra alternativa |
| **record** | anotación |
| **reducer** | reductor |
| **reel power lawn mower** | podadora de gasolina |
| **reeving** | aparejo |
| **refinished** | recabado |
| **refrigerant** | refrigerante |
| **regulated area** | área reglamentada |
| **regulation** | regla [REG-la] |
| **reinforcing steel** | acero de refuerzo |
| **reinforcing strip** | listón de refuerzo |
| **relay** | relevador, relé |
| **release** | liberador |
| **release mechanism** | mecanismo de desenganche |

| | |
|---|---|
| **remote valves** | válvulas de control remoto |
| **removal** | remoción |
| **rent piping** | tubería de ventilación |
| **repair** | reparación |
| **repeat of press** | falla en el mecanismo de cierre de la prensa |
| **repeat violation** | infracción repetida [in-frak-SYON re-pe-TI-da], violencia repetida [vi-o-LEN-sya re-pe-TI-da] |
| **replenish** | reponer |
| **report** | informe [in-FOR-me], reporte [re-POR-te] |
| **re-roofing** | reemplazo de tejado |
| **rescue** | Salvar [sal-VAR], rescatar [res-ca-TAR] |
| **reset circuit** | circuito reprogramado |
| **reshaping** | reformación |
| **residential construction** | construcción residencial |
| **resilient seal** | cierre clásico |
| **resistance** | resistencia |
| **respirator** | respirador |
| **respirator (mask)** | máscara respiradora [MAS-ka-ra res-pir- |

| | a-DO-ra] |
|---|---|
| **restoration** | restauración |
| **restraining cable** | cable de contención |
| **retaining wall** | muro de apoyo |
| **retarding chamber** | cámara retardadora |
| **retarding device** | dispositivo retardador |
| **retrieval system** | sistema de recuperación, sistema de recobrar |
| **return bend** | sifón |
| **return pipe** | tubo de retorno |
| **reusable air purifying respirator** | respirador purificador de aire re-usable |
| **reverse bend** | dobleces alternos |
| **reverse signal alarm** | alarma de retroceso [a-LAR-ma de re-tro-SE-so] |
| **revolving door** | alarma de retroceso, giratoria |
| **rewind** | dar cuerda |
| **ridge** | caballete |
| **riding lawn mower** | cortacésped, podadora |
| **rights** | derechos [de-RE-chos] |
| **rigid conduct** | conducto rígido |
| **rim** | borde |
| **ring** | anillo |
| **ring barker** | descortezador tipo anillo |

| | |
|---|---|
| **ring buoy** | boya salvavidas anular |
| **ring spinning frame** | telar para anillos |
| **ring test** | prueba de sonido por percusión |
| **rivet** | remache |
| **rock** | piedra |
| **rock drill** | perforadora de roca |
| **rod** | barra |
| **roller (grading)** | aplanadora |
| **roller (paint)** | rodillo |
| **rollover protective structure** | estructura de protección contra vuelco |
| **roof** | tejado |
| **-asphalt** | -asfalto |
| **-gable** | -inclinado |
| **-gambrel** | -abuhardillado |
| **-leak** | -gotera |
| **-saddle (2 sided)** | -a dos aguas |
| **-slate** | -empizarrado |
| **-tile** | -de tejas |
| **-tin** | -de estaño |
| **roof bracket** | palometa para techar |
| **roof car** | grúa de azotea |
| **roof car positioning device** | aparato de colocación para las grúas de azotea |
| **roof iron** | herraje para techo |
| **roof jack** | casquete de techo |
| **roofing** | instalación de |

| | |
|---|---|
| | tejado |
| **roofing bracket** | enganche, agarre para techo, palometa para techar |
| **rooftop** | azotea |
| **room** | cuarto |
| **rope** | soga/cuerda |
| **rope carrier** | ceñidor de suspensión |
| **rope support** | cuerda de retención |
| **rope washer** | lavadora de cuerda |
| **rotary blast cleaning table** | mesa giratoria para limpieza con rocío a presión |
| **rotary staple cutter** | cortadora giratoria de hebras |
| **rotating work platform** | plataforma rotatoria de trabajo |
| **rotten** | podrido |
| **rough** | áspero |
| **rough lumber** | madera bruta |
| **rough size** | tamaño bruto |
| **rough-in** | de mano gruesa |
| **round turn and a half hitch** | lazo de vuelta y media |
| **router** | buriladora, acanalador |
| **rove** | mechar |
| **roving parts** | piezas de mechar |
| **roving waste opener** | abridora de desperdicios de |

| | |
|---|---|
| | mechera |
| **rubber** | goma |
| **rubber grommet** | arandela de goma |
| **rubber mallet** | mazo de goma |
| **rubber mill** | laminadores de goma |
| **rubber slip end** | terminales de goma deslizable/ajustable |
| **rule** | regla [REG-la], norma [NOR-ma] |
| **run idle** | marchar al vacío |
| **rung (ladder)** | peldaño, escalón |
| **runner** | viga de apoyo |
| **runner coupler** | acoplador de viga de apoyo |
| **running ends** | extremos corredizos |
| **running overcurrent device** | dispositivo de sobre-corriente |
| **running rope (wire)** | cable portante |
| **runway (airport)** | pista |
| **rust** | oxido |
| **s/s** | fracción de segundo |
| **saber** | caladora eléctrica portátil |
| **saber saw** | sierra de vaivén |
| **saddle plates** | placa de apoyo |
| **saddles** | soporte |
| **safety** | seguridad [se-gu-ri-DAD] |
| **safety belt** | cinturón de seguridad [sin-tur-ON de se-gur-i- |

| | DAD] |
|---|---|
| **safety can** | envase de seguridad, recipiente de seguridad |
| **safety equipment** | equipo de seguridad [e-KI-po de se-gur-i-DAD] |
| **safety glasses** | lentes de seguridad, gafas, anteojos [an-te-O-hos] |
| **safety harness** | ásperas de seguridad [AS-per-as de se-gur-i-DAD], arnés de seguridad |
| **safety hazards** | riesgos a la seguridad, peligros a la seguridad |
| **safety helmet** | casco de seguridad |
| **safety latch** | pestillo de seguridad con resorte |
| **safety lights** | luz de seguridad |
| **safety line** | cuerda de seguridad |
| **safety line** | cuerda de seguridad |
| **safety net** | malla de seguridad [MA-ya de se-gur-i-DAD], red de seguridad [red de se-gur-i-DAD] |
| **safety relief capacity** | capacidad de |

| | descarga de la válvula de seguridad |
|---|---|
| **safety relief device** | dispositivo de seguridad |
| **safety relief lines** | tuberías de seguridad |
| **safety triprod** | varilla de embrague de seguridad |
| **safety valve** | válvula de seguridad |
| **safety vest** | chaleco de seguridad |
| **salary** | suelto |
| **salt** | sal |
| **salvage tank** | tanque de recuperación |
| **sampler** | tomador de muestras |
| **sampling** | muestra |
| **sand** | arena |
| **sandbag** | saco de arena |
| **sander** | lijadora |
| **sanding** | lijada |
| **sanitary land fill** | terreno en el que se cubre la basura con tierra |
| **sash gang saw** | sierra alternativa, sierra de vaivén |
| **sash window** | ventana de guillotina |
| **saw** | sierra |

| | |
|---|---|
| saw, electric | sierra eléctrica |
| sawdust | aserrín |
| sawhorse | burro, caballete |
| sawhorses | caballetes |
| sawzall® | sierra alternativa |
| scaffold | andamio |
| scaffold grade | de tipo para andamio |
| scaffold hitch | enganche del andamio, lazo de andamio |
| scaffolding | andamio, andamiaje |
| schedule | horario |
| schematic | esquemático |
| scrap | basura |
| screening exam | examen de clasificación |
| screening station | estación clasificadora |
| screw leg | pata de tornillo |
| scroll saw | sierra de contornear, sierra de marquetería |
| seat belt | cinturón de seguridad |
| self contained breathing apparatus operating in pressure demand or other positive pressure mode | equipo de respiración aparato otro tipo de presión positiva |
| self energizing band | freno de banda |

| | |
|---|---|
| **type brake** | auto-multiplicador de fuerza |
| **self energizing brake** | freno de auto-multiplicación de fuerza |
| **self powered platform** | plataforma automotriz |
| **self-closing, self-locking gate** | portón de cierre automático |
| **self-contained device** | dispositivos auto-contenidos |
| **self-contained pilot operated relief valve** | válvula de seguridad accionada por piloto integrado |
| **self-contained spring loader relief valve** | válvula de seguridad de tipo independiente con resorte |
| **self-rescue mouthpiece respirator** | boquilla para emergencia |
| **self-setting brake** | freno automático |
| **seniority status** | privilegio de antigüedad |
| **sensors** | detectores |
| **service panel** | tablero de servicio |
| **set** | juego |
| **sewage** | aguas de alcantarilla |
| **sewage system** | alcantarillado |
| **sewer** | alcantarilla |
| **shaft (crankshaft)** | cigüeñal |
| **shaft (pole,rod)** | barra, vara |
| **shaft (vertical air** | hueco, pozo |

| | |
|---|---|
| passage) | |
| shafting | conjunto de ejes |
| shakeout or conditioning tumbler | sacudidores o tambores para acondicionamiento |
| shank | palanca, mango |
| shape | forma |
| shaping | hacer moldura, moldear |
| sharp | afilado |
| sharpening stone | piedra de afilar |
| shear | fuerza |
| shear wall | muro sismo-resistente |
| shear-bolt | perno de madera |
| shearing machine | fundidora |
| shears | tijeras |
| sheathing | entablado |
| sheave | polea acanalada |
| shed | cobertizo |
| sheen | luminosidad |
| sheer panel | cabria |
| sheet | hoja |
| sheet (framing) | plancha |
| sheet metal | hojalata |
| sheet vinyl | de lamina de vinil |
| sheeting | lamina |
| sheetrock | panel de yeso |
| shelf | estante |
| shelf pin | clavija para estantes |
| shielding | soldadura por arco metálico protegido |

| | |
|---|---|
| shim | calza, cuna |
| shingle (asphalt) | teja de asfalto |
| shingling | para tablas |
| shiny | luminoso |
| ship scaffold | andamio de barco |
| shipbreaking | desguazar, rompe, destrozar barcos |
| shock loading | carga súbita |
| shock loads | cargas |
| Shockproof | anti-golpes |
| shoe type brake | freno de zapata |
| shore scaffold | andamio con puntal |
| shoring | apuntalamiento, equipo de soporte |
| shoring layout | plan de apuntalamiento, plan de equipo de soporte |
| short (height) | bajo |
| short (length) | corto |
| short circuit | poner en cortocircuito |
| shoulder harness | arnés de hombro |
| shovel | pala |
| shower | ducha |
| shredding machine | máquina de destrozar, desintegradora |
| shrink band | banda de sellar |
| shutoff switch | interruptor principal |
| shutoff valve | válvula de cierre |
| shutter | contraventana |

| | |
|---|---|
| shuttle | lanzadera |
| side | lado |
| side linged swinging type door | puerta de vaivén montada con bisagras hacia los lados |
| side pull | tracción lateral |
| side rail | larguero lateral |
| side-by-side | al lado |
| sidetrack | apartadero |
| sidewalk | acera |
| siding | revestimiento |
| silica (glass making) | sílice |
| silicone | silicona |
| silicone (as a general term for caulk) | masilla de calafateo |
| sill | antepecho |
| sill plate | placa de solera |
| singeing (burning) machine | chamuscadora |
| single cleat ladder | escalera sencilla de listones |
| single frame hammer | martillo pilón |
| single point adjustable suspension scaffold | andamio ajustable de suspensión sencilla |
| single stroke reset | programador de un recorrido completo |
| single trip | desechable |
| single use air purifying respirator | respirador mecánico desechable con purificador |

| | |
|---|---|
| | de aire |
| **single use dust respirator** | respirador mecánico desechable para polvo |
| **sink** | lavabo |
| **sintering** | aglutinación |
| **size** | tamaño |
| **size box** | tina de encolar |
| **size mixture** | cola |
| **skid tank** | tanques con largueros |
| **skids** | largueros |
| **skid-steer loader** | cargadora |
| **skill saw** | sierra circular |
| **skylight** | tragaluz, claraboya |
| **slab** | losa |
| **slab on grade** | losa sobre el suelo |
| **slash** | cuchillada, barra oblicua |
| **slate** | pizarra |
| **sledge** | almádena |
| **sledge hammer** | marrón, martillo de los monos |
| **sleeve bearings** | cojinete de rodadura (fricción) |
| **sleeve type flanges** | pestaña tipo tensora |
| **sliding cut-off saws** | sierras de cortar corredizas |
| **sliding door** | Puerta corrediza |
| **sliding trench shield protector** | deslizable para zanja |
| **sliding window** | corredera |

| | |
|---|---|
| **sling (for injured arm)** | cabestrillo |
| **sling (throwing)** | honda |
| **sling line** | eslinga de cola, línea para levantar o mover material |
| **slip joints** | juntas deslizantes |
| **slip tube** | tubo deslizable |
| **slitter knives** | cuchilla rajadora |
| **sliver** | cinta |
| **slop sink** | pileta para lavar |
| **slope** | cuesta |
| **slope (or) hill** | inclinación [in-klin-a-SYON] |
| **sloping system** | sistema de ángulo de inclinación |
| **slot** | ranura |
| **slot-type** | tipo ranura |
| **sludge door** | puerta para limpieza |
| **primers** | pinturas base |
| **smoke detector** | detector de humo |
| **smooth-pivoted idler role** | rodillo (pivotante / loco / de tensión de giro suave) |
| **snap tie** | tirante de resorte |
| **snaphook** | gancho de seguridad |
| **socket** | copa, receptáculo, bocabarra |
| **socket wrench** | llave de copa, herramienta de copa, llave de |

| | |
|---|---|
| | dados, herramienta de buje |
| **socketing** | encasquillar |
| **soffit** | sofito |
| **soft material** | terreno blando |
| **soil** | suelo, terreno tierra |
| **soil test** | prueba de suelo, prueba de terreno, prueba de tierra |
| **soil type** | tipo de suelo, tipo de terreno, tipo de tierra |
| **solar panels** | paneles solares |
| **soldered** | estaño - soldada |
| **soldered-brass** | soldadura con cautín |
| **soldering iron** | pistola de soldar |
| **soldering wire** | alambre soldadura |
| **solenoid valve coils** | bobinas de solenoide |
| **solid fuel salamander** | estufa de combustible sólido |
| **solvent** | disolvente |
| **sound engineering practices** | prácticas ingenieriles, de ingeniería correctas |
| **sound level meter** | medidor de niveles de sonido |
| **source material** | fuente de energía nuclear |
| **spar tree** | árbol guía |
| **spark** | chispa |

| | |
|---|---|
| spark arrestor | para-chispa |
| speeders | aceleradores |
| spigot | llave de paso |
| spike pole | bastón con espigón |
| spill | derrame |
| spin | hilar |
| spirometer | espirómetro |
| splice (to) | empalmar |
| splice plate | placa de empalme |
| split rail switch | interruptor de cambio de vía |
| split rim | aro partido |
| split side rail | larguera lateral partido |
| spoil pile | montón de material excavado |
| sponge | esponja |
| spool | devanar |
| spot welding | soldadura por punto |
| spotting projectile | proyectil para indicar posición de impacto |
| spout | boca de descarga |
| spray finishing | acabado por rocío |
| spray liquid heaters | calentadores para rociadores de líquido |
| sprayer | rociador |
| spraying | rocío |
| spreader (seed, etc.) | esparcidora |
| spreader beam | viga separadora |
| spring laded check | válvula de retención |

| | |
|---|---|
| valve | de resorte |
| sprocket | rueda dentada |
| spud wrench | llave de conector de acero |
| square | cuadrado [kwa-DRA-do] |
| square (tool) | escuadra |
| square feet | pies cuadrados |
| square inches | pulgadas cuadradas |
| squeeze pressure | presión de prensado |
| squeezer extractor | máquina exprimidora |
| squibs | mecha detonadora |
| stable rock | piedra estable |
| stacker | apiladora |
| stacking pin | pasador de apilar |
| stain | mancha |
| stain-glass window | vidriera |
| stairs | escaleras |
| stairway enclosure | caja de la escalera; hueco para la escalera |
| stairway railing | baranda de escalera |
| staking pad | amortiguador |
| stalled rotary current | pérdida de velocidad de la corriente del motor |
| stanchion | barra |
| standards | normas, reglas |
| standing rope | cable de soporte |
| standpipe | torre de suministro de agua |

| | |
|---|---|
| staple | grapa, mecha |
| staple gun | pistola de grapas |
| staples | grapas |
| static head | presión estática, carga estática |
| static head of the loading | presión estática de la carga |
| steam blasting | rocío por vapor |
| steam jackets | tapas a vapor |
| steel | hierro [YER-ro], acero [a-SER-o] |
| steel clevis | abrazadera de acero |
| steel construction | construcción en acero [kon-struk-SYON en a-SER-o] |
| steel joist | vigueta de acero |
| steel plate | plancha de acero |
| steel shackle | grillete de acero |
| steel shot | granalla de acero |
| steel strip | fleje de acero |
| steel wool | lana de acero |
| steel work | estructura de acero |
| stepladder | escalera baja |
| steps | escalones |
| sticker | listón separador |
| stiff boom | armadía flotante |
| stiff log derrick | de mástil rígido |
| stilts | zancos |
| stirrup | estribo |
| stitching | costura |
| stock chest | armario para el material |

| | |
|---|---|
| stonesetter | empedrador |
| stonework | empedrado |
| stop | umbral |
| stop bolt | perno limitador |
| stop device | dispositivo de parada |
| stops | inmovilizadores |
| storm door | contrapuerta |
| storm window | guardaventana |
| straight | recto |
| straight cup wheel | piedra de esmeril acopada cilíndrica |
| straight takeoff | toma de fuerza directa |
| straight wheel | piedra de esmeril cilíndrica |
| straightedge | Regla metálica |
| straight-graded | fibra derecha |
| strainers | coladores |
| strap | tira |
| strap (framing) | cubrejunta |
| strap hinge | bisagra de paleta |
| street | de calle |
| stress grade | grado de resistencia |
| string | hilo |
| string line | línea |
| stringer | larguero |
| stringing | tendido |
| stringing line | línea tendida |
| strip knives | cuchillas de recorte |
| stripper | separador |
| stripping roll | rodillo para |

| | desprender |
|---|---|
| **stroking selector** | selector de recorrido |
| **struck-by** | golpeado [gol-pe-A-do], impactado [im-pak-TA-do] |
| **structural grade aluminum** | aluminio de tipo estructural |
| **strut** | diagonal, soporte de suspensión, codal |
| **stucco** | estuco, concreto, repello |
| **subconductor** | conductor secundario |
| **substantive rules** | reglas substantivas |
| **sulky-type mower** | podadora tipo arado |
| **supply** | abastecimiento |
| **supply air respirator** | equipo de respiración con suministro de aire |
| **supply air respirator with full facepiece helmet or hood** | máscara completa, capacete o capucha con suministro de aire |
| **supply hose** | manguera de abastecimiento |
| **support operations** | operaciones de mantenimiento |
| **support pad** | almohadilla de soporte |
| **supporting bearer** | soporte de retención |
| **supporting cable** | cable de suspensión |

| | |
|---|---|
| **supporting member** | pieza de apoyo |
| **supporting steel** | soportes de acero |
| **supporting structures** | estructuras de apoyo |
| **supporting systems** | sistema de soporte |
| **supporting tie** | amarre de retención |
| **surface grinder machine** | pulidora, afiladora, de superficie esmeriladora |
| **surfacer** | máquina para acabado |
| **surging** | de crecimiento brusco de la presión |
| **suspended scaffold** | andamio de suspensión, a. voladizo |
| **suspension wire rope** | cable de suspensión |
| **swab** | palito con algodón, estropajo |
| **swing cut off saws** | sierras de cortar oscilantes |
| **swing frame grinder** | máquina esmeriladora con bastidor oscilante |
| **swing line** | tubería / línea flexible |
| **swing pipe** | tubo flexible |
| **swing radius** | radio de recorrido |
| **swinging scaffold** | guindola |
| **swivel joint** | unión giratoria |
| **swivelled double-bar-gate** | portillo giratorio de barrea doble |

| | |
|---|---|
| **symptomatology** | síntomas |
| **systemic infections** | infecciones sistemáticas |
| | |
| **tackle** | cuadernal |
| **tag (to) (tagging)** | etiquetar, rotular |
| **tag line** | cable de cola, cable de maniobra |
| **tagout** | interrupción de energía usando etiqueta [in-ter-rup-SYON de en-er-HI-a us-an-DO e-ti-KE-ta] |
| **tailing device** | dispositivo terminal |
| **takeup gear** | engranaje de tensión |
| **tamping** | apisonamiento |
| **tank car** | carro cisterna, vagones tanque |
| **tank motor vehicle** | vehículo tanque |
| **tank vessel** | buque tanque |
| **tape** | cinta |
| **tape (electrical)** | esparadrapo [es-pa-ra-DRA-po] |
| **tape measure** | cinta metro |
| **tape winding** | enrollado de cinta |
| **taper set** | tornillos o clavijas cónicas |
| **tapered takeoff** | toma de fuerza gradual |
| **tapper** | golpeador |

| | |
|---|---|
| **tar paper/roof underlayment** | refuerzo para techo |
| **temporary lighting** | alumbrado temporero |
| **tender frame** | armazón rama tersura |
| **tenoning** | espigadora |
| **tensile loading** | carga sometida a tracción |
| **tension device** | mecanismo de tracción |
| **terminal boxes** | caja de la terminal |
| **terminal landing** | descanso del terminal |
| **terminal screw** | tornillo de los terminales |
| **test vessel** | envase para prueba |
| **thimble** | manguito, guardacabo |
| **thread grinding wheel** | piedra de esmeril para rosca, de roscar, para hacer roscas |
| **three-way plug** | enchufe de tres puntas |
| **three-wire type** | tres conductores, tipo tres alambres |
| **threshold limit** | límites mínimos de concentración |
| **thrust outs** | almojaya / salientes |
| **tie (framing)** | traviesa |
| **tie (general)** | amarre |

| | |
|---|---|
| **tie ends** | retenedores en los extremos |
| **tie line** | línea de conexión |
| **tie rod** | barra tirante |
| **tieback** | cuerda de anclaje, viento de cuerda |
| **tieback** | viento de cuerda |
| **tiedowns** | inmovilizadores |
| **tie-off** | amarre, amarrarse, conectarse |
| **tight fitting chemical goggle** | gafa anti-química de ajuste hermético |
| **tightness** | opresión en el pecho |
| **tile (floor)** | loseta |
| **tile (roof)** | teja de arcilla |
| **tile (wall)** | azulejo |
| **tile cutter** | corta-baldosas |
| **tile nippers** | pinzas corta-azulejo |
| **tiled** | de losas |
| **time clock areas** | áreas de los relojes de control de entrada |
| **time weighted average** | concentración promedio en un tiempo determinado |
| **timer** | contador |
| **tin** | estaño |
| **tin (container/can)** | lata |
| **tin snips** | tijeras para hojalata |

| | |
|---|---|
| **tire rack** | porta-neumáticos |
| **toeboard** | tabla de capellada, pie, tablón de capellada |
| **tongs (large)** | tenazas |
| **tongs (small)** | pinzas |
| **tongue and grooved lumber** | madera machihembrada |
| **tongue and groove** | machihembrado, lengüeta y ranura |
| **tool** | herramienta [er-ra-MYEN-ta] |
| **toolbox** | caja de herramientas [KA-ha de er-ra-MYEN-tas] |
| **tools** | herramientas |
| **top plate** | placa superior |
| **torch (welding)** | soplete |
| **torque** | torsión |
| **torque wrench** | llave de torsión |
| **tow line** | cuerda de remolque |
| **towel** | toalla |
| **tower truck** | camión de torre |
| **towing** | remolque |
| **T-pipe** | tubo en T |
| **track** | vía |
| **track lights** | luces en rieles |
| **traffic cones** | conos de seguridad |
| **trailer** | remolque |
| **training** | entrenamiento [en-tren-a-MYEN-to], |

| | |
|---|---|
| **tramp iron** | fragmentos de hierro |
| **transformer** | transformador |
| **transistor** | transistor |
| **trap** | colectores |
| **trap (plumbing)** | sifón |
| **trapdoor** | trampa |
| **trash** | basura |
| **trash bag** | bolsa para basura |
| **trash can** | bote de basura |
| **traveling cable** | cable desplazable |
| **tray** | bandeja |
| **trench** | Trinchera [trin-CHE-ra], zanja [SAN-ha] |
| **trench box** | caja de trinchera |
| **trencher** | trinchador |
| **trenching** | zanjando; excavando |
| **trestle ladder** | escalera de caballete |
| **trestle ladder scaffold** | a. de escalera de caballete |
| **trim** | adorno |
| **trip** | desenganche, desembragar |
| **trip level** | niveles de desconexión |
| **tripping means** | mecanismo de desembrague |
| **trough** | artesa |
| **trowel** | paleta / allanadora |

| | |
|---|---|
| **trowel hawk** | llana enyesadura |
| **truck** | Camión |
| **truck crane** | remolque motorizado |
| **truck rear axle** | eje trasero de un camión |
| **trunnions** | soportes giratorios |
| **truss** | pieza de refuerzo |
| **tub** | tina |
| **tube** | tubo |
| **tube and coupler scaffold** | a. tubular con acopladores |
| **tube bender** | dobladora de tubos |
| **tubing loop** | anillo tubular |
| **tubular welded frame scaffold** | andamio de armazón tubular soldada |
| **tumbler** | tambor |
| **turnbuckles** | tensores |
| **turnover bar** | palanca de rotación |
| **twister** | torcedor |
| **two-hand trip** | desembrague a dos manos |
| **two-point suspension scaffold** | guindola, andamio de suspensión doble |
| **two-way voice communication system** | sistema de radio telefonía |
| **type "C" supplied air respirators, pressure-demand class** | equipo de respiración con suministro de aire tipo "C", a demanda de presión |

| | |
|---|---|
| **type "C" supplied-air respirators** | equipo de respiración con suministro de aire tipo "C" |
| **type "C" supplied-air respirators continuous flow** | equipo de respiración con suministro de aire tipo "C" de flujo continuo |
| **U-bolt clip** | grillete, grapa de perno en "U", grapa para cable |
| **ultimate strength** | resistencia final |
| **undercoating** | primera mano (de pintura) |
| **undercut** | rebaje |
| **underground** | subterráneo |
| **underlayment** | base del piso |
| **underpinning** | apuntalar |
| **undressed lumber** | madera sin cepillar |
| **unenclosed sides** | lados al descubierto |
| **uneven** | desigual |
| **unfinished** | sin terminar |
| **union** | Sindicato [sin-di-KA-to], unión [un-YON], unión laboral [un-YON labor-AL] |
| **union representative** | representante laboral [re-pre-sen- |

| | TAN-te la-bor-AL] |
|---|---|
| **unitized tooling** | troquel herramienta unificada |
| **unpierced wall** | pared sin agujeros |
| **unpressurized (open bell)** | a presión ambiente (campana abierta) |
| **unprotected edge** | borde expuesto, borde descubierto |
| **unprotected side** | lado expuesto, lado descubierto |
| **unstable** | Inestable |
| **unstable material** | terreno inestable |
| **unstable soil** | suelo inestable, terreno inestable, |
| **unstrading** | destrenzado |
| **uplift** | levantamiento |
| **upright (scaffold)** | montante (andamios) |
| **upsetters** | recalcaduras |
| **upstream** | corriente ascendente |
| **user-compounder** | usuario que mezcla explosivos o agentes detonantes |
| **utility knife** | cuchilla para uso general |
| | |
| **vaccum collapse** | colapso por vacío, compresión, comprimir |
| **vaccum gauge** | manómetro de vacío |
| **vacuum** | aspiradora |

| | |
|---|---|
| valley | valle |
| valley (roof) | lima hoya |
| valve | válvula |
| valve protecting cap | tapa protectora de la válvula |
| valve seat | asiento de la válvula |
| valve spud | conexión de la válvula |
| valve stem | vástago de la válvula |
| vaporizer-burner | vaporizador |
| vapor-tight seal | sello hermético al vapor |
| vault (architectural) | bóveda |
| vent (air, gas) | conducto |
| vent cap | tapa para respiradores, para ventilación |
| vent piping | tapa para respiradores, tubería para ventilación, tubería de escape |
| ventilation | ventilación, extracción |
| venting (of safety relief devices) | desfogar, ventear, descargar (válvulas de seguridad) |
| vertical grinder | esmeriladora vertical, pulidora |
| vertical slip form | vertical, afiladora vertical |
| vest | chaleco [cha-LE- |

| | |
|---|---|
| | ko] |
| **view port** | puerto de vigilancia |
| **vinyl** | vinilo |
| **violation** | infracción [in-frak-SYON], violación [vi-o-la-SYON] |
| **vise** | prensa de tornillo |
| **vise-grip pliers** | alicates de presión |
| **visual test** | prueba visual |
| **volt** | voltio |
| **V-shaped arrangement** | aparejo en V |
| **vulcanized** | |
| | |
| **wagon crane** | grúa vagón |
| **walk-behind power lawn mower** | cortacésped, podadora de rodadura |
| **walk-in closet** | vestidor, ropero empotrado |
| **wall** | pared |
| **wall to wall** | muro a muro |
| **wall to wall (carpet)** | moqueta |
| **warning symptoms** | avisos de precaución |
| **warp** | torcimiento |
| **warper** | urdidor |
| **washed cotton** | algodón lavado |
| **washing machine** | lavadora |
| **waste pipe** | desagüe |
| **waste valve** | Válvula de desagüe |
| **water** | Agua |
| **water gels** | gelatina acuosa |

| | |
|---|---|
| **water seal** | cierre a prueba de agua, cierre hidráulico |
| **water slurry explosive** | explosivo de suspensión acuosa |
| **watt** | vatio |
| **weak cement** | cemento de poca resistencia |
| **weak roof-to-shell seam** | costura débil del techo al casco |
| **wearing surface** | superficie de desgaste |
| **weather shelter** | techado |
| **web** | alma, vigueta |
| **wedge socket type fastening** | sujetador tipo casquillo cuña |
| **weed burners** | quemador de maleza |
| **weedwaker** | desyerbador |
| **weighted distance** | distancia ponderada |
| **weight-loaded relief valve** | válvula de seguridad de contrapeso |
| **welder** | soldador |
| **welding** | soldadura |
| **welding helmet** | careta de soldar |
| **welding leads** | cable eléctrico para soldar |
| **welding or brazing** | soldadura dura o blanda, bronce-soldadura, cobre-soldadura, |

| | |
|---|---|
| | soldadura fuerte, soldadura con aleación de cobre |
| **wet** | mojado |
| **wet lap pulp** | hojas plegadas de pasta húmeda |
| **wet method** | método mojado/ método húmedo |
| **wet standpipe system** | sistema de columna de alimentación de agua |
| **wet test meter** | medidor de gas húmedo |
| **wet-dry vac** | aspiradora de agua |
| **wharf** | descargador |
| **wharfman** | operador del descargador |
| **What is your last name?** | ¿Cuál es su apellido? [kwal es su a-pay-YI-da?] |
| **What is your name?** | ¿Como se llama? [KO-mo se YA-ma?], ¿Cuál es su nombre? [kwal es su NOM-bre?] |
| **wheel** | rueda |
| **wheel brakes** | freno de rueda |
| **wheel drive** | accionamiento de las ruedas |
| **wheel stops** | dispositivo inmovilizador para neumático |

| | |
|---|---|
| **wheelbarrow** | carretilla[kar-re-TI-ya] |
| **wheeled extinguishers** | extinguidores sobre ruedas; sobre carritos |
| **whipline** | torno sencillo |
| **whirlpool** | Jacuzzi |
| **whole body clothing** | vestimenta que cubra el cuerpo |
| **width** | anchura |
| **winch (crank)** | manivela |
| **winch (hoist)** | cabestrante |
| **winch (move with...)** | mover con un cabestrante |
| **winch head** | cabezal del torno |
| **window** | Ventana |
| **window jack** | andamio de palometa de ventana |
| **window jack scaffold** | andamio de palometa en ventana, andamio de escala para limpiar ventanas |
| **window sill** | alfeizar |
| **window unit** | -unidad de ventana |
| **wire center cord** | centro de cable, cuerda con alma |
| **wire conductor** | conductor |
| **wire rope clip** | grillete, grapa de perno en "U", grapa para cable |

| | |
|---|---|
| **wire tie** | viento de alambre |
| **wire-winding** | enrollado de alambre |
| **wiring** | alambrado |
| **withdrawal lines** | tuberías de extracción, tuberías de salida |
| **wood pole scaffold** | andamio de poste de madera |
| **wood splice plates** | viga maestra de empalme |
| **wooden bracket form scaffold** | andamio de palometa de gato, andamio de palometa, andamio para carpinteros |
| **wooden bracket form scaffold** | andamio con soporte de madera, andamio para carpinteros, andamio de palometa, andamio de palometa de gato |
| **wooden punch** | vara de madera |
| **woodpecker type** | tipo pica madera |
| **woodshaper** | talladora |
| **work activity** | actividad laboral |
| **work practice** | método para realizar el trabajo |
| **work vest** | chaleco de trabajo |
| **worker** | trabajador (male) [tra-ba-ha-DOR]; / |

| | |
|---|---|
| | trabajadora (female) [tra-ba-ha-DOR-a] |
| working conditions | condiciones laborales [kon-di-si-ON-es la-bor-AL-es] |
| working deck | plataforma de trabajo |
| working length | longitud útil |
| working load | carga de trabajo |
| working pressure | presión de operación |
| work-lead circuit | circuito conductor eléctrico |
| workplace | lugares de trabajo [lu-GAR-es de tra-BA-ho], planta de trabajo [PLAN-ta de tra-BA-ho] |
| worsted drawing | peinado de lana pura |
| wrench | llave |
| wrench (adjustable) | llave Inglesa |
| wringer extractor | máquina exprimidora |
| yard (lumber, etc.) | astillero, maderería |
| yard-arm-doorway | puerta de tranca |
| yarn manufacturing | manufactura de hilaza |
| yield(to) | fundir |
| yield point | límite de elasticidad/fluencia |

**zero cut (carved steel)**     tallado de acero

# SPANISH TO ENGLISH

EASY REFERENCE

# DICTIONARY

# SPANISH → ENGLISH DICTIONARY

| | |
|---|---|
| a presión (campana cerrada) | pressurized (closed bell) |
| a presión ambiente (campana abierta) | unpressurized (open bell) |
| andamio de escalera de caballete | trestle ladder scaffold |
| andamio tubular con acopladores | tube and coupler scaffold |
| aire acondicionado central | -a/c central |
| abanderado | flagman |
| abastecimiento | supply |
| abolladura | cratering |
| abrasivo fuerte | hard deep-cutting abrasives |
| abrazadera | clamp |
| abrazadera de acero | steel clevis |
| abrazadera de anclaje al | rail clamps |

|  |  |
|---|---|
| **carril** | |
| **abrazadera diagonal** | diagonal bracing |
| **abrelatas** | can opener |
| **abridora de desperdicios de mechera** | roving waste opener |
| **acabado** | finish (of a surface) |
| **acabado por rocío** | spray finishing |
| **acceso a la salida** | exit access |
| **accesorio, conector** | fitting |
| **accionamiento de las ruedas** | wheel drive |
| **aceite** | oil |
| **aceleradores** | speeders |
| **acepilladora, cepillo, lijadora** | planer |
| **acera** | sidewalk |
| **acero de mayor resistencia** | plow steel |
| **acero de refuerzo** | reinforcing steel |
| **acero dúctil** | mild steel |
| **acero forjado** | drop forged steel |
| **acero sin galvanizar** | black steel |
| **acoplador automático de cierre rápido** | automatic quick-closing coupling |
| **acoplador de viga de apoyo** | runner coupler |
| **acoplar, cuñas para martillo** | key |
| **actividad laboral** | work activity |

| | |
|---|---|
| **acueducto** | city main |
| **adaptador** | adapter |
| **adhesiva** | adhesive |
| **administración [ad-min-is-tra-SYON], gerencia[he-REN-sya]** | management |
| **adorno** | trim |
| **afilado** | sharp |
| **agente de enlace** | bonding agent |
| **agente detonante** | blasting agent |
| **agitador de cilindro** | cylinder shaker |
| **aglutinación** | sintering |
| **aglutinante** | binder |
| **Agua** | water |
| **aguas de alcantarilla** | sewage |
| **agujero** | hole (small) |
| **aire [AY-ray]** | air |
| **aire acondicionado** | air conditioning |
| **aire limpio** | makeup air |
| **aislamiento [ais-la-MYEN-to]** | insulation |
| **aislamiento de R veinte [ER-ray VAIN-tay]** | R-20 insulation |
| **al lado** | side-by-side |
| **alambrado** | wiring |
| **alambre de conexión** | bond wire |
| **alambre soldadura** | soldering wire |
| **alarma de retroceso [a-LAR-ma de re-tro-SE-so]** | reverse signal alarm |

| | |
|---|---|
| **alarma de retroceso, giratoria** | revolving door |
| **albañilería [al-ban-yi-le-RI-a]** | masonry |
| **alcantarilla** | culvert |
| **alcantarilla** | sewer |
| **alcantarillado** | sewage system |
| **alfeizar** | window sill |
| **alfombra** | carpet |
| **algodón esterilizado en el autoclave** | autoclaved cotton |
| **algodón lavado** | washed cotton |
| **alicates** | pliers |
| **alicates de presión** | vise-grip pliers |
| **alicates para cortar cables** | pliers (lineman's) |
| **alma, vigueta** | web |
| **almádena** | sledge |
| **almohadilla de soporte** | support pad |
| **almohadillas** | padders |
| **almojaya / salientes** | thrust outs |
| **altera los tejidos, artefactos** | artifacts |
| **altura de la zona de respiración** | breathing zone height |
| **altura sobre pilares de hormigón, altura del muelle** | pier height |
| **alumbrado temporero** | temporary lighting |
| **aluminio** | aluminum |
| **aluminio de tipo** | structural grade |

| | |
|---|---|
| **estructural** | aluminum |
| **amarre** | bonding |
| **amarre** | tie (general) |
| **amarre de retención** | supporting tie |
| **amarre, amarrarse, conectarse** | tie-off |
| **amasadores de rodillo cruzado** | cross role brakes |
| **amoníaco anhidro** | anhydrous ammonia |
| **amortiguador** | staking pad |
| **ampliación** | addition (building) |
| **anchura** | width |
| **anclaje** | anchor |
| **anclaje** | anchorage |
| **andamiaje, anclaje** | bracing |
| **andamio** | scaffold |
| **andamio ajustable de suspensión múltiple (para albañiles)** | mason's adjustable multiple-point suspension scaffold |
| **andamio ajustable de suspensión sencilla** | single point adjustable suspension scaffold |
| **andamio colgante** | float scaffold |
| **andamio colgante para interiores** | interior hung scaffold |
| **andamio con base cuadrada para albañiles** | bricklayer's square scaffold |

| | |
|---|---|
| andamio con puntal | shore scaffold |
| andamio con soporte de madera | wooden bracket form scaffold |
| andamio de área grande | large area scaffold |
| andamio de armazón tubular soldada | tubular welded frame scaffold |
| andamio de barco | ship scaffold |
| andamio de caballete, andamio de burros | horse scaffold |
| andamio de escala para limpiar ventanas, andamio de palometa en ventana | window jack scaffold |
| andamio de espiga, andamio de parihuela | needle beam scaffold |
| andamio de molde | form scaffold |
| andamio de molde con palometa de metal | metal bracket form scaffold |
| andamio de palometa de gato | pump jack scaffold |
| andamio de palometa de gato, andamio de palometa, andamio para carpinteros | wooden bracket form scaffold |
| andamio de palometa de ventana | window jack |
| andamio de palometa en ventana, andamio de escala para limpiar ventanas | window jack scaffold |
| andamio de palometa, andamio de escala | jack scaffold |
| andamio de palometas en | ladder jack |

| | |
|---|---|
| **escalera** | scaffold |
| **andamio de palometas para carpintero, andamio con soportes para carpinteros** | carpenters bracket scaffold |
| **andamio de poste** | pole scaffold |
| **andamio de poste de madera** | wood pole scaffold |
| **andamio de poste de madera independiente** | independent pole scaffold |
| **andamio de silla mecedora** | boatswain's chair scaffold |
| **andamio de suspensión, a. voladizo** | suspended scaffold |
| **andamio de yesero** | plasterer's scaffold |
| **andamio para decorador** | decorator scaffold |
| **andamio reclinado** | lean to scaffold |
| **andamio voladizo** | outrigger scaffold |
| **andamio, andamiaje** | scaffolding |
| **andén** | foot walk |
| **anexo, que pertenece a** | appurtenant |
| **angular** | angle |
| **angular de metal** | metal angle |
| **anillo** | ring |
| **anillo de reducción** | bushing |
| **anillo tubular** | tubing loop |
| **anotación** | record |
| **antepecho** | sill |
| **anti-golpes** | Shockproof |
| **aparato** | apparatus |

| | |
|---|---|
| aparato de aire acondicionado | a/c wall unit |
| aparato de aviso de proximidad | proximity warning device |
| aparato de colocación para las grúas de azotea | roof car positioning device |
| aparatos de suministro | dispensing device |
| aparejo | reeving |
| aparejo en V | V-shaped arrangement |
| apartadero | sidetrack |
| apelar [a-pel-AR] | appeal |
| apellido [a-pe-YI-do] | last name |
| apéndice, adiciones, añadiduras | addenda |
| apiladora | stacker |
| apisonamiento | tamping |
| aplanadora | roller (grading) |
| aprobar [a-pro-BAR] | approve |
| apuntalamiento, equipo de soporte | shoring |
| apuntalar | underpinning |
| arandela de goma | rubber grommet |
| arandelas/selladores de juntas | gaskets and thread sealants |
| árbol guía | spar tree |
| arbusto | bush |
| área al descubierto | open floor area |

| | |
|---|---|
| área reglamentada | regulated area |
| áreas de los relojes de control de entrada | time clock areas |
| arena | sand |
| armadía flotante | stiff boom |
| armadía, brazo de grúa | boom |
| armadura, marco | framing |
| armario para el material | stock chest |
| armazón rama tersura | tender frame |
| arnés de hombro | shoulder harness |
| arnés del cuerpo | body harness |
| aro partido | split rim |
| artesa | trough |
| artesano de banco, del lado del horno de coque | benchman, coke side |
| artesano del banco, del lado de empuje | benchman, pusher side |
| asbesto | asbestos |
| aserrín | sawdust |
| asfalto | asphalt |
| asfalto con penetración 300 | penetration asphalt (300) |
| asiento de la válvula | valve seat |
| ásperas de seguridad [AS-per-as de se-gur-i-DAD], arnés de seguridad | safety harness |
| áspero | rough |
| aspiradora | vacuum |
| aspiradora de agua | wet-dry vac |
| astilladora | chipper |
| astillas para pasta papelera | pulp chips |

| | |
|---|---|
| astillero, maderería | yard (lumber, etc.) |
| atomizadores electrostáticos | electrostatic atomizing head |
| autopista, carretera | highway |
| autorizar [auw-to-ri-SAR] | authorize |
| avance lento | jog |
| avellanado | countersunk |
| aviso preliminar | pre action system |
| avisos de precaución | warning symptoms |
| azadón | hoe |
| azotea | rooftop |
| azulejo | tile (wall) |
| B- para vapores gaseosos orgánicos tipo barbilla | B- organic vapor gas mask chin - style |
| baches | potholes |
| bajo | short (height) |
| bala | bale |
| balanza | balance |
| balaustres | baluster |
| bancada | press bed |
| banda de sellar | shrink band |
| bandeja | tray |
| bandeja recoge-gotas | drip pan |
| bañera, tina | bathtub |
| baranda | guardrail |
| baranda | railing |
| baranda de escalera | stairway railing |
| baranda para colisión | crashrail |

| | |
|---|---|
| barra | rod |
| barra | stanchion |
| barra de agarre | grab rail |
| barra guía cuchilla | blade guide rod |
| barra tirante | tie rod |
| barra, vara | shaft (pole,rod) |
| barrena terrena | power auger (ground) |
| barreno de detonación | blast hole |
| barrera | barrier |
| barril | kegs |
| barril giratorio | barrel |
| base de apoyo | footing |
| base de los estabilizadores | floats |
| base del piso | underlayment |
| bastón con espigón | spike pole |
| basura | scrap |
| basura | trash |
| batería | battery |
| batidora horizontal | horizontal dough mixer |
| bayeta | duster |
| bencina | benzin (benzine) |
| biela | crank arm |
| bilirrubina | bilirubin |
| bisagra | hinge |
| bisagra de paleta | strap hinge |
| bloque de apoyo | bearing block |
| bloque de rama derecha | isolated right |

| | |
|---|---|
| **(aislado)** | bundle branch block |
| **bloque de relleno** | filler block |
| **bloque de unión** | coupler block |
| **bobinas de solenoide** | solenoid valve coils |
| **boca** | bungs |
| **boca de descarga** | spout |
| **bolsa para basura** | trash bag |
| **bolsa para los clavos** | nail pouch |
| **bolsillo de aire viciado** | dead air pocket |
| **bomba** | pump |
| **bomba de desplazamiento positivo (bomba volumétrica)** | positive displacement pump |
| **bomba personal para tomar muestra** | personal sampling pump |
| **bomba reforzadora de presión** | booster pump |
| **boquilla de llenado** | fill spout |
| **boquilla metálica** | metal horns |
| **boquilla para emergencia** | self-rescue mouthpiece respirator |
| **borde** | rim |
| **borde expuesto, borde descubierto** | unprotected edge |
| **Bordillo** | curb |
| **borra de algodón** | cotton waste |
| **bote de basura** | trash can |
| **bóveda** | vault (architectural) |

| | |
|---|---|
| **boya salvavidas anular** | ring buoy |
| **brea de alquitrán de hulla** | coal for pitch |
| **brecha, grieta** | opening (in wall, etc.) |
| **brocha** | brush (painting) |
| **buque tanque** | tank vessel |
| **bureta pequeña** | midget bubbler |
| **buriladora, acanalador** | router |
| **burro, caballete** | sawhorse |
| **C- cartucho para vapores gaseosos orgánicos colocada en el pecho o sobre la espalda** | C- organic vapor gas mask canister front or back mounted |
| **caballetes** | sawhorses |
| **cabestrillo** | sling (for injured arm) |
| **cabezal** | header, cross head |
| **cabezal del torno** | winch head |
| **cabezales formados al calor** | hot-formed heads |
| **cabezales formados en frío** | cold-formed heads |
| **cabida** | occupant load |
| **cabina de mando** | controller cabinets |
| **cable** | cable |
| **cable conductor de electrodo** | electrode lead cable |

| | |
|---|---|
| cable de cola, cable de maniobra | tag line |
| cable de contención | restraining cable |
| cable de soldar en espiral | coiled welding cable |
| cable de soporte | standing rope |
| cable de suspensión | supporting cable |
| cable desplazable | traveling cable |
| cable eléctrico para soldar | welding leads |
| cable portante | running rope (wire) |
| cables de arranque | jumper cables |
| cables de maniobra, sogas de operación | operating ropes |
| cabo de mecha | bult |
| cabrestante de cadena | hoisting tackle (chain) |
| cabria | sheer panel |
| cabria de parapeto | breast derrick |
| cabria rotativa de vientos | guy derrick |
| caída de objetos, objetos volantes | falling objects |
| caída de presión | pressure drop |
| caja de ángulos | miter box |
| caja de herramientas | toolbox |
| caja de la escalera; hueco para la escalera | stairway enclosure |
| caja de la terminal | terminal boxes |
| caja de techo | ceiling box |
| caja de trinchera | trench box |

| | |
|---|---|
| **caja portátil para zanja** | portable trench box |
| **caladora eléctrica portátil** | saber |
| **calafateo** | caulking |
| **calandrias, máquina para dar brillo (lustre) a telas, papel, etc. (material pasa entre dos rodillos)** | calenders |
| **calderas abiertas para freír con grasa** | open fat kettles |
| **caldera** | furnace |
| **calefacción** | heating |
| **calefacción por inducción de agua caliente** | hot-water radiant heating |
| **calefacción, ventilación y aire acondicionado** | HVAC |
| **calentador del agua** | heater, hot-water |
| **calentador del agua** | hot-water heater |
| **calentadores para rociadores de líquido** | spray liquid heaters |
| **calibrador** | caliper |
| **calza, cuna** | shim |
| **calzado para descarrilamiento** | derail block |
| **calzo para choques** | bumber block |
| **cámara** | chamber |
| **cámara de ionización de bolsillo** | pocket chamber |
| **cámara en J** | J- box |
| **cámara retardadora** | retarding |

| | |
|---|---|
| | chamber |
| **cámaras de aire comprimido** | caissons |
| **Camión** | truck |
| **camión de pre-mezclado, mezcla-lista** | ready-mix truck |
| **camión de torre** | tower truck |
| **camión industrial [kam-YON in-dus-TRYAL]** | powered industrial truck |
| **camión tanque** | motor vehicle cargo tank |
| **camiones móviles de abastecimiento** | mobile supply trucks |
| **camioneta** | pickup truck |
| **camisa exterior** | jacket (mixer) |
| **campana de cubierta** | enclosing hood |
| **campana de gas** | gas bell |
| **campana de techo** | canopy hood |
| **campana de techo** | overhead canopy hood |
| **canales horizontales** | horizontal channel |
| **canaleta, canalón** | gutter |
| **canasta** | basket |
| **canasto para elevar, elevador de cangilones** | bucket elevator |
| **capa** | coat (layer) |
| **capacidad de descarga de la válvula de seguridad** | safety relief capacity |
| **capacidad vital (FVC)** | forced vital capacity |
| **cara combada** | crown face |

| | |
|---|---|
| carbón de piedra | coal |
| cardar | card |
| careta de soldar | welding helmet |
| carga calculada | rated load |
| carga contraviento | mild loading |
| carga de trabajo | working load |
| carga máxima designada | maximum intended load |
| carga sometida a tracción | tensile loading |
| carga súbita | shock loading |
| carga suspendida libremente, carga de suspensión libre | freely suspended load |
| cargador delantero | front-end loader |
| cargadora | skid-steer loader |
| cargas | shock loads |
| carretilla elevadora de gran alcance | high lift rider truck |
| carretilla[kar-re-TI-ya] | wheelbarrow |
| carro cisterna, vagones tanque | tank car |
| carro para enfriar maní | peanut cooling truck |
| cartel | poster |
| cartucho | primer |
| cartuchos | canister |
| cartuchos con cebo | primed cartridges |
| cartuchos detonantes | detonating primers |

| | |
|---|---|
| casas | houses |
| casco | hard hat |
| casco de seguridad | safety helmet |
| casquete de techo | roof jack |
| casquillo | ferrule |
| casquillo acopado | cupback bushing |
| casquillo detonador (fulminante) | blasting cap |
| casquillos de grampas | clam caps |
| catástrofe [ka-TAS-tro-fe] | catastrophe |
| acero de refuerzo [a-SER-o de re-FWER-so] | rebar |
| cebo | primer |
| cemento | cement |
| cemento de poca resistencia | weak cement |
| cenizas | burns |
| centro | center |
| centro de cable, cuerda con alma | wire center cord |
| ceñidor de suspensión | rope carrier |
| cepillo | brush (cleaning) |
| cepillo mecánico | jointer |
| cerca | fence |
| cerradura | lockset |
| chaleco [cha-LE-ko] | vest |
| chaleco de seguridad | safety vest |
| chaleco de trabajo | work vest |
| chaleco salvavidas [cha-LE-ko sal-va-VI-das] | life jacket |
| chamuscadora | singeing |

|  |  |
|---|---|
| | (burning) machine |
| cheque | check |
| chimenea | chimney, fireplace |
| chispa | spark |
| chivo | claw |
| chorro de agua | loaded stream |
| cierre a prueba de agua, cierre hidráulico | water seal |
| cierre clásico | resilient seal |
| cierre para el compresor | compressor cutoff |
| cierre para la | booster cutoff |
| cigüeñal | shaft (crankshaft) |
| cilindro superior | pressure roll |
| cimiento | foundation |
| cincel, escoplo | chisel |
| cinta | tape |
| cinta adhesiva protectora | masking tape |
| cinta de ajuste para la cabeza | headband |
| cinta del freno | brake locks |
| cinta metro | tape measure |
| cinta para juntas | joint tape |
| cinta para medir [SIN-ta PA-ra ME-dir], cinta metro [SIN-ta ME-tro] | measuring tape |
| cinta pescadora | fish tape |
| cinturón de seguridad | seat belt |

| | |
|---|---|
| **circuito** | circuit |
| **circuito abierto** | open-circuit, open wire |
| **circuito conductor eléctrico** | work-lead circuit |
| **circuito de cierre** | interlocking circuitry |
| **circuito de decisión** | decision making circuitry |
| **circuito de mando** | control circuit |
| **circuito reprogramado** | reset circuit |
| **citación [si-ta-SYON]** | citation |
| **cito- tóxico** | cytotoxic |
| **cizalles para lingotes** | billet shears |
| **clavadora de armazón** | nailgun, framing |
| **clavadora neumática para pisos** | nailgun, flooring |
| **clavadora neumática para techar** | nailgun, roofing |
| **clavija** | plug (male connector to electrical socket) |
| **clavija de conexión** | attachment cap |
| **clavija para estantes** | shelf pin |
| **cobertizo** | shed |
| **cobre** | copper |
| **cocedor para encolar, cocedor** | cooker |

| | |
|---|---|
| código | code |
| código de construcción | building code |
| codo | elbow |
| cojinete de rodadura (fricción) | sleeve bearings |
| cola | size mixture |
| coladores | strainers |
| colapso por vacío, compresión, comprimir | vaccum collapse |
| colectores | trap |
| colectores de alimentación | portable outlet leaders |
| colectores metálicos | metal combs |
| collar central | core collar |
| collarín | central hub |
| color | color |
| columna | column |
| combustible | fuel |
| combustible diesel | diesel fuel |
| compactador | compactor |
| compañía [kam-pan-YI-a], empresa [em-PRE-sa] | company |
| compresor | compressor |
| compuesto de juntas | joint compound |
| compuesto para tubos | pipe-joint compound |
| comunicación de riesgos [ko-mu-ni-ka-SYON de ri-ES-gos] | hazard communication |
| concentración de partículas suspendida en el aire | airborne concentration |

| | |
|---|---|
| concentración promedio en un tiempo determinado | time weighted average |
| concreto | concrete |
| condensador | condenser |
| condiciones críticas | deep seated condition |
| condiciones laborales [kon-di-si-ON-es la-bor-AL-es] | working conditions |
| conducto | pipe, channel, conduit |
| conducto de ventilación | vent |
| conducto de metal | conduit (metal) |
| conducto de PVC | conduit (PVC) |
| conducto rígido | rigid conduct |
| conductor | wire conductor |
| conductor secundario | subconductor |
| conector de alambre aplastado | connector, crimp |
| conexión a tierra para brindar protección | protective ground |
| conexión de la válvula | valve spud |
| conexión de mando de la barra distribuidora | operating bus linkage |
| confluencias | junctions |
| conglomerado, agregado | aggregate |
| conjunto de ejes | shafting |
| conmutadores colgantes | pendant push button |
| conocimiento [ko-no-si-MYEN-to] | knowledge |
| conos | cones |

| | |
|---|---|
| conos de seguridad | traffic cones |
| construcción | contruction |
| construcción en acero [kon-struk-SYON en a-SER-o] | steel construction |
| construcción residencial | residential construction |
| contador | timer |
| contrapuerta | storm door |
| contraventana | shutter |
| control automático de protección | fail-safe control |
| control para alta velocidad | overhead governor |
| copa cerrada (punto de inflamación) | closed cup (flash point) |
| copa, receptáculo, bocabarra | socket |
| copla | coupling |
| cordón de tiza | chalkline |
| correa de polea (escalonada) | cone-pulley belt |
| corrección [ko-rek-SYON] | abatement |
| corredera | sliding window |
| corredores | path of travel |
| corriente ascendente | upstream |
| corriente descendente | downstream |
| corta-baldosas | tile cutter |
| cortacésped, podadora | riding lawn mower |
| cortacésped, podadora de rodadura | walk-behind power lawn mower |

| | |
|---|---|
| cortado | pre-cut |
| cortador de ramas | pruners |
| cortadora de diagonales | diagonal cutter |
| cortadora giratoria de hebras | rotary staple cutter |
| corto | short (length) |
| costura | stitching |
| costura débil del techo al casco | weak roof-to-shell seam |
| criba separadora | grader |
| cristal, hoja, vidrio marcado | pane (window) |
| cromatografía de gas | gas chromatography |
| cruceta, refuerzo transversal | cross brace |
| cuadernal | tackle |
| cuadernal desplazable | load black |
| cuadrado [kwa-DRA-do] | square |
| cuarto | quart |
| cuarto | room |
| cubeta | bucket |
| cubierta | cover |
| cubiertos de enchufes, Placas de pared | outlet covers (wall plates) |
| cubrejunta | strap (framing) |
| cubre-zapatos | overshoes |
| cuchilla | blade |
| cuchilla para uso general | utility knife |
| cuchilla rajadora | slitter knives |
| cuchilla raspadora | doctor blades |

| | |
|---|---|
| cuchillada, barra oblicua | slash |
| cuchillas de recorte | strip knives |
| cuchillo | knife |
| cuerda de anclaje, viento de cuerda | tieback |
| cuerda de remolque | tow line |
| cuerda de retención | rope support |
| cuerda de seguridad | safety line |
| cuerda de seguridad [KWER-da de se-gu-ri-DAD] | lifeline |
| cuerda de seguridad [KWER-da de se-gu-ri-DAD], cordón [kor-DON], pila [PI-la] | lanyard |
| cuerda detonante | cordeau detonant fuse |
| cuerda, soga, cable, soguería | guy |
| cuerdas de mano | hand line |
| cuesta | slope |
| cumplir [kum-PLIR] | comply |
| cuña saliente (chaveta) | projecting key |
| cuña tipo travesaño | bunk block |
| curso | course |
| dar cuerda | rewind |
| de afuera | outdoor |
| de brida, reborde, pestaña | flanged |
| de calle | street |
| de crecimiento brusco de la presión | surging |
| -de cuarenta pies | -40' |

| | |
|---|---|
| de desagüe | drain |
| -de dieciséis pies | -16' |
| -de diez pies | -10' |
| de extracción | exhaust |
| de lamina de vinil | sheet vinyl |
| de laminado | laminate |
| de losas | tiled |
| de mano gruesa | rough-in |
| de mástil rígido | stiff log derrick |
| -de seis pies | -6' |
| de tipo para andamio | scaffold grade |
| -de treinta y dos pies | -32' |
| -de veinticuatro pies | -24' |
| -de veintiocho pies | -28' |
| deficiente en oxígeno [de-fi-SEN-te de ok-SI-he-no], nivel bajo de oxígeno [ni-VEL BA-ho de ok-SI-he-no] | oxygen deficient |
| deflector | baffle |
| del extremo | end |
| del garaje | garage |
| demanda de presión | pressure demand |
| demostrar | demonstrate |
| departamento | department |
| deposición | deposition |
| depósito de aire comprimido | air receiver |
| depósito de gas | gas holder |
| depósitos, tanques | portable tanks |

| | |
|---|---|
| **portátiles** | |
| **derechos [de-RE-chos]** | rights |
| **derrame** | spill |
| **desagüe** | waste pipe |
| **desarrollar** | develop |
| **desatascador, sopapa** | plunger (toilet) |
| **descanso** | break (lunch) |
| **descanso** | landing |
| **descanso del terminal** | terminal landing |
| **descargador** | wharf |
| **descortezador tipo anillo** | ring barker |
| **desechable** | single trip |
| **desembrague a dos manos** | two-hand trip |
| **desenganche, desembragar** | trip |
| **desfibrado de algodón, deshilado de algodón** | garnetting |
| **desfogar, ventear, descargar (válvulas de seguridad)** | venting (of safety relief devices) |
| **desgaste** | attrition |
| **desguazar, rompe, destrozar barcos** | shipbreaking |
| **deshiladuras de trapo** | frayed cloth |
| **deslizable para zanja** | sliding trench shield protector |
| **destrenzado** | unstrading |
| **desviación máxima del muelle** | maximum spring deflection |
| **desyerbador** | weedwaker |
| **detector de humo** | smoke detector |

| | |
|---|---|
| detectores | sensors |
| detonador eléctrico | electric blasting cap |
| devanar | spool |
| diagonal, soporte de suspensión, codal | strut |
| diluyente de pintura | paint thinner |
| dinero | money |
| dirección [di-rek-SYON], domicilio [do-mi-SIL-yo] | address |
| director | director |
| disciplina | discipline |
| disciplinario | disciplinary |
| discrimen, discriminación | discrimination |
| diseño | design |
| disolvente | solvent |
| dispositivo alimentador de correa | belt-feed device |
| dispositivo automático de sobrecarga | automatic overload device |
| dispositivo de accionamiento | initiating device |
| dispositivo de parada | stop device |
| dispositivo de seguridad | safety relief device |
| dispositivo de sobre-corriente | running overcurrent device |
| dispositivo inmovilizador | locking device |
| dispositivo inmovilizador para neumático | wheel stops |

| | |
|---|---|
| **dispositivo mecánico eficaz** | positive mechanical device |
| **dispositivo para conectar a tierra** | positive grounding device |
| **dispositivo retardador** | retarding device |
| **dispositivo terminal** | tailing device |
| **dispositivo volcadura del recipiente para electrolitos** | carboy tilter |
| **dispositivos auto-contenidos** | self-contained device |
| **distancia ponderada** | weighted distance |
| **disyuntor con candado, candado** | padlock |
| **división** | division |
| **dobladora de chapas** | press brakes |
| **dobladora de tubos** | tube bender |
| **doble** | double |
| **dobleces alternos** | reverse bend |
| **documento** | document |
| **dosímetro anular** | film ring |
| **dosímetro de bolsillo** | pocket dosimeter |
| **dosímetro fotográfico personal** | film badge |
| **drenaje** | drainboard |
| **ducha** | shower |
| **duchas de seguridad de lluvia artificial intensa** | deluge showers |

| | |
|---|---|
| dueño [DWEN-yo] | owner |
| edificio | building |
| eje central | core shaft |
| eje de la polea matriz | head pulley shaft |
| eje trasero de un camión | truck rear axle |
| electrodoméstico, aparato | appliance |
| elemento de alimentación manual | manual input |
| elemento de extracción | output element |
| elemento para la selección de graduación | mode selection element |
| elevadores para personal, elevadores para trabajadores | manlift |
| embalse, área de retención | impounding basin |
| embrague | clutch |
| empalmar | splice (to) |
| empedrado | stonework |
| empedrador | stonesetter |
| en T (tay) | fittting-T |
| en Y (ee-gree-ay-gah) | fitting-Y |
| encargados de la armadía | boom men |
| encasquillar | socketing |
| encendedor de mecha | fuse igniter |
| encendedores | igniters |
| encerramiento, protector cerrado | enclosure |
| enchufe de 120 (ciento veinte) voltios | outlet, 120v |
| enchufe de 240 (doscientos | outlet, 240v |

| | |
|---|---|
| cuarenta) voltios | |
| enchufe de tres puntas | three-way plug |
| encofrados | forms |
| energía a gran velocidad | high-energy-rate |
| enfermedad | disease |
| enfermedad (es) [en-fer-me-DAD / en-fer-me-DAD-es] | illness (es) |
| enfermedad pulmonar | chest illness |
| enganche del andamio, lazo de andamio | scaffold hitch |
| enganche, agarre para techo, palometa para techar | roofing bracket |
| engranaje de tensión | takeup gear |
| enrollado de alambre | wire-winding |
| enrollado de cinta | tape winding |
| ensamblar | abut (to) |
| entablado | sheathing |
| entallador | notcher |
| entrenamiento [en-tren-a-MYEN-to], | training |
| entrevista [en-tre-VIS-ta] | interview |
| envase de seguridad, recipiente de seguridad | safety can |
| envase para prueba | test vessel |
| envases portátiles para repartir agua | portable drinking water dispensers |
| envoltura de material resistente al agua y al | house wrap (water & wind |

| viento | resistant) |
|---|---|
| equipo de contragolpe | counterblow equipment |
| equipo de halar o jalar | pulling ring |
| equipo de protección personal [e-KI-po de pro-tek-SYON per-son-AL] | personal protective equipment |
| equipo de respiración | self contained breathing |
| equipo de respiración auto contenido de circuito abierto | open circuit self-contained breathing apparatus |
| equipo de respiración auxiliar auto-contenido | auxiliary self contained breathing apparatus |
| equipo de respiración con suministro de aire | supply air respirator |
| equipo de respiración con suministro de aire tipo "C" | type "C" supplied-air respirators |
| equipo de respiración con suministro de aire tipo "C" de flujo continuo | type "C" supplied-air respirators continuous flow |
| equipo de respiración con suministro de aire tipo "C", a demanda de presión | type "C" supplied air respirators, pressure- |

| | |
|---|---|
| | demand class |
| equipo de respiración de circuito abierto auto-contenido | open circuit self-contained breathing apparatus |
| equipo de respiración purificador de aire | air purifying respirator |
| equipo de seguridad [e-KI-po de se-gur-i-DAD] | safety equipment |
| equipo elaborador procesador | process equipment |
| equipo para empaque o almacenaje | packing or storage aids |
| equipo pesado | heavy equipment |
| eritema | erythema |
| errores | mistakes |
| escala de gato; rampa de entrada (aserraderos) | jack ladder |
| escalera | ladder |
| escalera baja | stepladder |
| escalera de caballete | trestle ladder |
| escalera doble de listones | double cleat ladder |
| escalera fija, escala fija | fixed ladder |
| escalera mecánica | moving stairways |
| escalera portátil [es-ka-LE-ra] | ladder (portable) |
| escalera sencilla de listones | single cleat ladder |
| escaleras | stairs |

| | |
|---|---|
| **escaleras de escape, de salida** | exit stairs |
| **escalones** | steps |
| **escape de explosión** | explosion venting |
| **escombro** | debris |
| **escotilla** | hatchway |
| **escuadra** | square (tool) |
| **eslinga de cola, línea para levantar o mover material** | sling line |
| **esmeriladora vertical, pulidora** | vertical grinder |
| **esmeriladora, pulidora, afiladora, trituradora** | grinder |
| **espacio** | clearance, gap |
| **espacio abierto** | open space |
| **espacio cerrado para limpieza a presión con abrasivos** | abrasive blasting enclosure |
| **espacio libre** | clear |
| **espacio superior, espacio adecuado, margen de altura mínima** | headroom |
| **espacios intermedios entre habitaciones** | intervening room spaces |
| **espacios ocupados** | occupancies |
| **esparadrapo [es-pa-ra-DRA-po]** | tape (electrical) |
| **esparcidora** | spreader (seed, etc.) |
| **espátula** | putty knife |
| **espigadora** | tenoning |

| | |
|---|---|
| espirómetro | spirometer |
| esponja | sponge |
| esquemático | schematic |
| esquina | corner (outside) |
| esquinal | knee brace |
| estabilizadores | outriggers |
| establecimiento [es-tab-le-si-MYEN-to] | establishment |
| estación clasificadora | screening station |
| estampadora, impresora | printing machine |
| estampar en relieve | embosser |
| estándar primario | primary standard |
| estante | shelf |
| estaño | tin |
| estaño - soldada | soldered |
| estirador de alfombras | carpet stretcher |
| estirar | draw |
| estribo | stirrup |
| estribos para viguetas | joist hanger |
| estructura de acero | steel work |
| estructura de protección contra vuelco | rollover protective structure |
| estructuras de apoyo | supporting structures |
| estuco, concreto, repello | stucco |
| estufa de combustible sólido | solid fuel salamander |

| | |
|---|---|
| etiqueta [e-ti-KE-ta] | label |
| etiquetar, rotular | tag (to) (tagging) |
| examen de clasificación | screening exam |
| exámenes para ubicación | preplacement |
| excavador trasera | backhoe |
| excavadora de hoyos | posthole-digger |
| exceso de rocío | overspray |
| exhibir, mostrar | display |
| explosivo de suspensión acuosa | water slurry explosive |
| explosivos instantáneos | high explosives |
| exterior | exterior |
| extinguidores sobre ruedas; sobre carritos | wheeled extinguishers |
| extremos corredizos | running ends |
| extrusión, estirado a presión | extrusions |
| fabricado | Prefabricated |
| falla en el mecanismo de cierre de la prensa | repeat of press |
| felpa | felt |
| fertilizante | fertilizer |
| fibra de vidrio | fiberglass |
| fibra derecha | straight-graded |
| fijar en posición de abierto | locked out |
| filtro | filter, cartridge |
| fleje de acero | steel strip |
| flota de calidad | grout float |
| fluorescente | flourescente |

| | |
|---|---|
| fondo doble | false bottom |
| forjado de latas a medidas exactas | can coining |
| forma | shape |
| formado | preformed |
| foso para el producto digerido | blow pit |
| fracción de segundo | s/s |
| fragmentos de hierro | tramp iron |
| frecuencia de banda central en ciclos por segundo | band center frequency in cycles per second |
| freno | brake |
| freno automático | self-setting brake |
| freno de auto-multiplicación de fuerza | self energizing brake |
| freno de banda auto-multiplicador de fuerza | self energizing band type brake |
| freno de rueda | wheel brakes |
| freno de zapata | shoe type brake |
| freno para decelerar | drag brake |
| fresadoras, torno (metal) | mills |
| fuente de energía | power pack |
| fuente de energía nuclear | source material |
| fuente para lavado de ojos | eye flushes |
| fuerza | shear |
| fuga (de combustible) | lead (fuel) |

| | |
|---|---|
| **fundente** | flux |
| **fundición en troquel para estereotipo** | die casting steoreotyping |
| **fundidora** | shearing machine |
| **fundir** | yield |
| **fundir (sobre soldadura), flujo** | flux |
| **fusible de encendido** | fuse lighters |
| **fusión** | fused |
| **gabinete** | cabinet |
| **gafa anti-química de ajuste hermético** | tight fitting chemical goggle |
| **galerías** | lofts |
| **gancho** | hook, hanger, peg |
| **gancho de seguridad** | snaphook |
| **gancho para tubos** | hanger (pipe) |
| **ganchos para cuadros** | picture hooks |
| **garrafón** | carboy |
| **gas** | gas (for heating) |
| **gas licuado de petróleo** | liquified petroleum gas |
| **gasolina** | gas (for vehicle) |
| **gasolina [gas-o-LI-na]** | gasoline |
| **gato** | jack (lifter) |
| **gelatina acuosa** | water gels |
| **generador de emergencia** | generator, backup |

| | |
|---|---|
| **generador intermitente** | batch type generator |
| **golpeado [gol-pe-A-do], impactado [im-pak-TA-do]** | struck-by |
| **golpeador** | tapper |
| **goma** | rubber |
| **gotera** | leak (pipe) |
| **gradación, preparaci6n del terreno** | grading |
| **grado de resistencia** | stress grade |
| **granalla de acero** | steel shot |
| **grano transversal** | cross-grain |
| **grapa, mecha** | staple |
| **grapadora martillo** | hammer tacker (stapler) |
| **grapas** | staples |
| **grapas contra-rechazador** | nonkick back dogs |
| **grava** | gravel |
| **grieta** | crack (wood,wall) |
| **grillete de acero** | steel shackle |
| **grillete, grapa de perno en "U", grapa para cable** | U-bolt clip |
| **grillete, grapa de perno en "U", grapa para cable** | wire rope clip |
| **grúa de azotea** | roof car |
| **grúa de pórtico** | gantry crane |
| **grúa puente** | overhead crane |
| **grúa vagón** | wagon crane |
| **guantes** | gloves |
| **guarda [WAR-da],** | guard |

resguardo [res-WAR-do]

| | |
|---|---|
| guardaventana | storm window |
| guía | guide (for door) |
| guía de onda abierta | open wave guide |
| guía manual, timón manual | hand steering wheel |
| guindola | swinging scaffold |
| guindola, andamio de suspensión doble | two-point suspension scaffold |
| gusanillo de taladro | auger-bit |
| habitaciones para vestirse | change rooms |
| hacer moldura, moldear | shaping |
| hemoglobinopatías | hemoglobinopthies |
| hendiduras | gouges |
| herraje para techo | roof iron |
| herramienta [er-ra-MYEN-ta] | tool |
| herramienta de émbolo/pistón accionada por martillo | hammer operated piston tool |
| herramienta eléctrica de mano | portable electric tool |
| herramienta eléctrica de pintura | power painting device (paint sprayer) |
| herramienta neumática | pneumatic powered tool |

| | |
|---|---|
| herramientas | tools |
| herramientas para sujetar accionadas por explosivos | explosion actuated fastening tool |
| hidruro de fenilo | phenyl hydrade |
| hierro [YER-ro], acero [a-SER-o] | steel |
| hierro de fundición gris | gray cast iron |
| hierros curvos | leg irons |
| higiene (higienista) industrial male: [I-jyen in-dus-TRYAL], female: [i-jyen-IS-ta in-dus-TRYAL] | industrial hygiene (ist) |
| higiene [I-jyen] | hygiene |
| hilar | spin |
| hilo | string |
| hoja | sheet |
| hojalata | sheet metal |
| hojas plegadas de pasta húmeda | wet lap pulp |
| honda | sling (throwing) |
| hora | hour |
| horario | schedule |
| hormigonera | cement mixer |
| hoyo | hole (small) |
| hoyo para poste | pole hole |
| hueco [WE-ko] | hole (in ground) |
| hueco, pozo | shaft (vertical air passage) |
| huella acanalada | hollow pan |

| | |
|---|---|
| | type thread |
| **imponer [im-po-NER** | enforce |
| **imprimador** | printer |
| **impulsor de fijadores** | fastener driver |
| **impulsor de línea** | linear actuators |
| **inclinación [in-klin-a-SYON]** | slope (or) hill |
| **indicador** | gauge |
| **indicador de contornos** | contour gauge |
| **indicador en caja de fibra de vidrio** | fiberglass box guide |
| **individual** | individual |
| **inestable** | unstable |
| **infecciones sistemáticas** | systemic infections |
| **informe [in-FOR-me], reporte [re-POR-te]** | report |
| **infracción [in-frak-SYON], violación [vi-o-la-SYON]** | violation |
| **infracción intencionada [in-frak-SYON in-ten-syon-A-da], infracción intencional [in-frak-SYON in-ten-syon-AL]** | willful violation |
| **infracción repetida [in-frak-SYON re-pe-TI-da], violencia repetida [vi-o-LEN-sya re-pe-TI-da]** | Repeat violation |
| **ingresos** | Income |
| **inhalar [in-al-AR], aspirar [as-pir-AR]** | inhalation |
| **inmovilizador mecánico** | mechanical |

| | |
|---|---|
| | stop |
| **inmovilizadores** | stops |
| **inmovilizadores** | tiedowns |
| **inspección de verificación [in-spek-SYON de ve-ri-fi-CA-syon], inspección de seguimiento [in-spek-SYON de se-gi-MYEN-to]** | follow-up inspections |
| **inspeccionar [in-spek-syon-AR]** | inspect |
| **instalación de blanqueo continuo** | continuous bleaching range |
| **instalación de mercerización** | mercerizing range |
| **instalación de tejado** | roofing |
| **instalación principal** | head rig |
| **instrucciones** | instructions |
| **interrumpir con fusible, disyuntor con fusible** | fuse disconnect switch |
| **interrupción de energía usando candado y etiqueta [in-ter-rup-SYON de en-er-HI-a us-AN-do kan-DA-do i e-ti-KE-ta]** | lockout/tagout |
| **interrupción de energía usando candado, cierre de corriente, disyuntor** | lockout |
| **interrupción de energía usando etiqueta [in-ter-rup-SYON de en-er-HI-a us-an-DO e-ti-KE-ta]** | tagout |

| | |
|---|---|
| **interruptor automático** | breaker |
| **interruptor de cambio de vía** | split rail switch |
| **interruptor de circuito con pérdida a tierra [in-ter-rup-TOR de sir-KI-to kon PER-di-da a TYER-ra] , interruptor a tierra / fallo [in-ter-rup-TOR a TYER-ra / FA-yo]** | ground-fault circuit interrupter (GFCI) |
| **interruptor de seguridad** | limit switch |
| **interruptor para corte a baja temperatura, interruptor de cierre a baja temperatura** | low temperature shutoff switch |
| **interruptor principal** | shutoff switch |
| **investigación [in-ves-ti-ga-SYON]** | investigation |
| **irritantes industriales** | mechanical irritants |
| **Jacuzzi** | whirlpool |
| **juego** | set |
| **junta** | joint |
| **juntas deslizantes** | slip joints |
| **jurisdicción [hu-ris-dik-SYON** | jurisdiction |
| **lado** | side |
| **lado expuesto, lado descubierto** | unprotected side |
| **lados al descubierto** | unenclosed sides |

| | |
|---|---|
| ladrillo | brick |
| lamina | sheeting |
| laminadores de goma | rubber mill |
| lámpara con extensión | extension light |
| lámpara, luz | light fixture |
| lana de acero | steel wool |
| lanzadera | shuttle |
| larguera lateral partido | split side rail |
| larguero | stringer |
| larguero intermedio (andamio), baranda del medio, madero intermedio | middle rail (scaffold) |
| larguero intermedio, baranda del medio, madero intermedio | midrail |
| larguero lateral | side rail |
| largueros | skids |
| lata | tin (container/can) |
| lavabo | sink |
| lavadora | washing machine |
| lavadora de cuerda | rope washer |
| lazo de vuelta y media | round turn and a half hitch |
| lechada | grout |
| lechada, relleno, mezcla de cemento | grout |
| lecho fluidificado | fluidized bed |
| lentes de seguridad | goggles |
| lentes de seguridad, gafas, anteojos [an-te-O-hos] | safety glasses |

| | |
|---|---|
| lesión (es) [le-SYON / le-SYON-es] | injury (ies) |
| leucopenia | leukopenia |
| levantamiento | uplift |
| ley | law |
| lezna | awl |
| liberador | release |
| lijada | sanding |
| lijadora | sander |
| lijadora de correa | belt sander |
| lima | file |
| lima hoya | valley (roof) |
| límite de elasticidad/fluencia | yield point |
| límites mínimos de concentración | threshold limit |
| limpieza a presión con abrasivos | abrasive blasting |
| línea | line |
| línea | string line |
| línea de conexión | tie line |
| línea de gas | gas line |
| línea de guía | guideline |
| línea eléctrica | powerline |
| línea tendida | stringing line |
| linóleo | linoleum |
| linterna | flashlight |
| linterna de batería | electric safety flashlight |
| linterna eléctrica | electric safety lantern |
| lista de cotejo, lista de | check list |

**control**

| | |
|---|---|
| listón de refuerzo | reinforcing strip |
| listón de relleno | filler strip |
| listón separador | sticker |
| llana enyesadura | hawk (for drywall compound) |
| llana enyesadura | trowel hawk |
| llave | key |
| llave Allen | Allen key |
| llave de agua | Faucet |
| llave de conector de acero | spud wrench |
| llave de copa, herramienta de copa, llave de dados, herramienta de buje | socket wrench |
| llave de paso | spigot |
| llave de torsión | torque wrench |
| llave de trinquete | ratchet wrench |
| llave Inglesa | Allen (adjustable) wrench |
| locomotora de oruga | crawler locomotive |
| longitud útil | working length |
| los extremos de los cables de izar que no se enrollan en tambores | non drums end of the hoisting ropes |
| losa | paver |
| losa | slab |
| losa sobre el suelo | slab on grade |
| loseta | tile (floor) |

| | |
|---|---|
| loso de desplante | deck (subfloor) |
| luces en rieles | track lights |
| lugares de trabajo [lu-GAR-es de tra-BA-ho], planta de trabajo [PLAN-ta de tra-BA-ho] | workplace |
| luminosidad | sheen |
| luminoso | shiny |
| luz de seguridad | safety lights |
| machihembrado, lengüeta y ranura | tongue and groove |
| madera bruta | rough lumber |
| madera contrachapada, laminada | plywood |
| madera dura | hardwood |
| madera machihembrada | tongue and grooved lumber |
| madera para pasta papelera | pulpwood |
| madera sin cepillar | undressed lumber |
| madero colocado en las patas de los andamios para darles apoyo o sostén | mud sill |
| madero pesado | heavy timber |
| malacates operados manualmente | manually operated winches |
| malla de seguridad [MA-ya de se-gur-i-DAD], red de seguridad [red de se-gur-i- | safety net |

| | |
|---|---|
| malla protectora | enclosing screen |
| mancha | stain |
| mando magnético | magnetic controller |
| manera de desconectar, forma de desconectar, mecanismo de desconectar | disconnecting means |
| manguera | hose |
| manguera de abastecimiento | supply hose |
| manguito, guardacabo | thimble |
| manómetro de vacío | vaccum gauge |
| manufactura de hilaza | yarn manufacturing |
| máquina [MA-ki-na] | machine (n) |
| máquina con soporte de piso | bench stand machine |
| máquina con soporte de piso | floor stand machine |
| máquina de destrozar, desintegradora | shredding machine |
| máquina de estirado | drawing frame |
| máquina de labrar paneles | panel raiser |
| máquina esmeriladora con bastidor oscilante | swing frame grinder |
| máquina exprimidora | squeezer extractor |
| máquina exprimidora | wringer extractor |
| máquina para acabado | surfacer |

| | |
|---|---|
| **marchar al vacío** | run idle |
| **marco** | casing (window and door) |
| **margen de altura mínima desde el chasis hasta la carretera** | minimum road clearance |
| **marrón, martillo de los monos** | sledge hammer |
| **martillo** | hammer |
| **martillo chivo** | claw hammer |
| **martillo de forja** | drop hammer |
| **martillo de forja de armazón abierto** | open frame hammer |
| **martillo de mano para forjar, destajador** | blacksmith hammer |
| **martillo macizo** | heavy mass hammer |
| **martillo neumático** | jack hammer |
| **martillo pilón** | single frame hammer |
| **martillo rompe-concreto** | concrete breaker |
| **martinete de caída libre con plancha de madera** | board (drop) hammer |
| **mascara** | face shield |
| **máscara antigás con cartucho colocado en el pecho o sobre la espalda** | gas mask, front or back mounted canister |
| **máscara completa con filtro de gran eficacia** | high efficiency filter respirator |

| | |
|---|---|
| **máscara completa, capacete o capucha con suministro de aire** | supply air respirator with full facepiece helmet or hood |
| **máscara para vapores orgánicos** | organic vapor gas mask |
| **máscara purificadora de aire motorizada** | full facepiece powered air purifying respirator |
| **máscara respiradora [MAS-ka-ra res-pir-a-DO-ra]** | respirator (mask) |
| **masilla** | putty |
| **masilla de calafateo** | silicone (as a general term for caulk) |
| **mástil-guía** | gin pole |
| **materia pulverizada, polvo** | powder |
| **material** | material (substance) |
| **material de albañilería** | masonry material |
| **material que se presume contiene asbesto** | presumed asbestos containing material (PACM) |
| **mazo** | mallet |
| **mazo de goma** | rubber mallet |
| **mecanismo auxiliar de** | final terminal |

| | |
|---|---|
| **detención final** | stopping device |
| **mecanismo de control** | operating device |
| **mecanismo de desembrague** | tripping means |
| **mecanismo de desenganche** | release mechanism |
| **mecanismo de tracción** | tension device |
| **mecanismo para engranaje de la carga** | load engaging means |
| **mecha detonadora** | squibs |
| **mechar** | rove |
| **mechazos, tiros fallados** | misfires |
| **medidas** | measurements |
| **medidor con bureta** | large bubble meter |
| **medidor de gas húmedo** | wet test meter |
| **medidor de gas seco** | dry gas meter |
| **medidor de niveles de sonido** | sound level meter |
| **medidor de profundidad** | depth gauge |
| **medios de salida a nivel** | level egress components |
| **medios de salida inclinados** | inclined egress components |
| **mercurio** | Hg |
| **mesa giratoria para limpieza con rocío a presión** | rotary blast cleaning table |
| **metal** | metal |

| | |
|---|---|
| metal de aportación | filler metal |
| método | maneuver |
| método mojado/ método húmedo | wet method |
| método para realizar el trabajo | work practice |
| metro [ME-tro] | meter |
| mezcla de algodón | cotton blend |
| mezclas inflamables de vapor con aire | flammable vapor-air mixtures |
| microscopio corriente | light-field techniques |
| milímetro digital | digital multimeter |
| modelado, conformar | forming |
| modo de salida [MO-do de sa-LI-da] | means of egress |
| moho [MO-oh] | mildew |
| mojado | wet |
| moldura | molding |
| moldura de sillas | chair rail molding |
| moldura del techo | rake board |
| moldura para la cornisa | crown molding |
| moldura para los cuadros | picture rail |
| mono | coveralls |
| montacargas | dumbwaiter |
| montacargas | forklift |
| montacargas para elevar, carretilla elevadora | lift truck |
| montacargas, carretilla de | fork truck |

| | |
|---|---|
| **horquilla** | |
| **montante (andamios)** | upright (scaffold) |
| **montante para sostener el cabezal** | Jack (trimmer) |
| **montantes oprimidos** | indented mullions |
| **montón de material excavado** | spoil pile |
| **moqueta** | wall to wall (carpet) |
| **mortero, mezcla** | mortar |
| **motón de caja de bolas** | ball bearing block |
| **motón encasquillado** | bushed block |
| **motor** | motor |
| **motores primarios** | prime movers |
| **moto-sierra** | chainsaw |
| **muestra** | sampling |
| **muestras al azar** | grab samples |
| **multa [MUL-ta]** | penalty |
| **multar [mul-TAR]** | penalize |
| **muro a muro** | wall to wall |
| **muro de apoyo** | retaining wall |
| **muro sismo-resistente** | shear wall |
| **nafta de hulla** | coal naptha |
| **nivel de acción** | action level |
| **nivel de sonido medido en la escala A** | A-weighted sound level |
| **nivel máximo de la presión de sonido** | peak sound pressure level |
| **niveladora** | bulldozer |

| | |
|---|---|
| niveles de desconexión | trip level |
| normas, reglas | standards |
| nudo de presilla | bowline knot |
| objetos salientes | projection hazard |
| obligatorio [ob-li-ga-TOR-yo] | mandatory |
| ocupacional [o-ku-pa-SYON-al], laboral [la-bor-AL], en el trabajo [en el tra-BA-ho] | occupational |
| operación de picar | chipping operation |
| operaciones de mantenimiento | support operations |
| operador de carro de templar | quenching car operator |
| operador de máquina del lado del coque | machine operator, coke side |
| operador del descargador | wharfman |
| opresión en el pecho | tightness |
| orificio de salida | port |
| ornamento de techo | ceiling fixture |
| otro tipo de presión positiva | operating in pressure demand or other positive pressure mode |
| oxidantes aglutinados | caked oxidizers |
| oxido | rust |
| oxígeno [ok-SI-he-no] | oxygen |

| | |
|---|---|
| pabellón de descarga | discharge stack |
| pala | shovel |
| pala mecánica | power shovel |
| palanca | crowbar |
| palanca de gancho | peavys |
| palanca de rotación | turnover bar |
| palanca elevadora de costales | bag-arm elevator |
| palanca excavadora | digging bar |
| palanca, mango | shank |
| paleta | paddler |
| paleta / allanadora | trowel |
| palito con algodón, estropajo | swab |
| palo de almojaya | putlog |
| palometa | bracket |
| palometa de gato, escala de gato | pump jack bracket |
| palometa de presión | clip-on bracket |
| palometa para techar | roof bracket |
| panel | panel |
| panel de interruptores automáticos | breaker panel |
| panel de yeso | sheetrock |
| paneles solares | solar panels |
| para tablas | shingling |
| para-chispa | spark arrestor |
| pararrayos | flash arrester |
| parcela | Lot |
| pared | wall |
| pared circundante | confining wall |

| | |
|---|---|
| pared sin agujeros | unpierced wall |
| parquet (tarima de madera ensamblada) | parquet |
| parrilla de alta tensión | high-voltage grid |
| parte | part |
| parte delantera | front |
| partes de vapor o gas por cada millón de partes de aire contaminado por volumen a 25°C y 760 mm de presión Hg (mercurio) | p.p.m.-parts of vapor or gas per million parts of contaminated air by volume at 25°C and 760 mm Hg pressure |
| partición | partition |
| pasador de apilar | stacking pin |
| pasador de chaveta | cotter pin |
| pasador de eje | gudgeon |
| pasamano, baranda | handrail |
| pasillos de salida, pasadizos de escape | fire aisles |
| paso alterno, sin interferir con | bypassing |
| pata (andamio) | leg (scaffold) |
| pata de cabra | pry bar |
| pata de tornillo | screw leg |
| patrón | pattern template |
| pedazo | piece |
| pegamento, goma | glue |

| | |
|---|---|
| **peinado de lana pura** | worsted drawing |
| **peinadora para algodón** | cotton combers |
| **peines** | combs |
| **peines de entrecruce** | intersecting faller |
| **peldaño hueco de extremo abierto** | open end hollow rung |
| **peldaño, escalón** | rung (ladder) |
| **peligro** | danger |
| **peligro inminente [pe-LI-gro in-mi-NEN-te]** | imminent danger |
| **peligroso** | dangerous |
| **perdida de audición [per-DI-da de auw-di-SYON]** | hearing loss |
| **pérdida de velocidad de la corriente del motor** | stalled rotary current |
| **perforaciones** | digs |
| **perforadora de roca** | rock drill |
| **periodo de corrección [per-YO-do de ko-rek-SYON]** | abatement period |
| **permiso requerido [per-MI-so re-ke-RI-do]** | permit required |
| **perno de madera** | shear-bolt |
| **perno limitador** | stop bolt |
| **pernos de anclaje** | anchor bolts |
| **persona [per-SO-na]** | person |
| **persona cualificada [per-SO-na kwa-li-fi-CA-da]** | qualified person |
| **persona encargada de fijar el telar** | loom fixer |
| **pestaña guía** | driving flange |

| | |
|---|---|
| **pestaña tipo tensora** | sleeve type flanges |
| **pestillo de seguridad con resorte** | safety latch |
| **pico** | pick |
| **piedra** | rock |
| **piedra de afilar** | sharpening stone |
| **piedra de esmeril acopada cilíndrica** | straight cup wheel |
| **piedra de esmeril cilíndrica** | straight wheel |
| **piedra de esmeril para rosca, de roscar, para hacer roscas** | thread grinding wheel |
| **piedra estable** | stable rock |
| **pies cuadrados** | square feet |
| **pieza de anclaje** | hold-down |
| **pieza de apoyo** | supporting member |
| **pieza de encaje** | housing member |
| **pieza de refuerzo** | truss |
| **pieza de tela** | batt |
| **piezas de cierre** | breaching parts |
| **piezas de mechar** | roving parts |
| **piezas oscilantes** | reciprocating components |
| **pila** | pile |
| **pileta para lavar** | slop sink |
| **piloto** | pilot light |
| **pintura** | paint |
| **pinturas base** | primers |

| | |
|---|---|
| pinzas | tongs (small) |
| pinzas corta-azulejo | tile nippers |
| piso | flooring |
| piso falso | false floor |
| piso, suelo | floor |
| pista | runway (airport) |
| pistola de calafateo/selladora | calk gun |
| pistola de grapas | staple gun |
| pistola de soldar | soldering iron |
| pistón, émbolo | ram |
| pizarra | slate |
| placa de apoyo | saddle plates |
| placa de empalme | splice plate |
| placa de solera | sill plate |
| placa pectoral | breast plate |
| placa porta-estampa | bolster plate |
| placa superior | top plate |
| plan de apuntalamiento, plan de equipo de soporte | shoring layout |
| plancha | board, sheet (framing) |
| plancha de acero | steel plate |
| plancha de metal | metal plate |
| plano | plan (drawing) |
| planta de trabajo [PLAN-ta de tra-BA-ho], lugar de trabajo [lu-GAR de tra-BA-ho] | place of employment / workplace |
| plataforma [plat-FOR-ma] | platform |
| plataforma automotriz | self powered |

| | platform |
| --- | --- |
| **plataforma de descanso** | landing platform |
| plataforma de detención | catch platform |
| **plataforma de extensión** | extension platform |
| plataforma de hormigón, de concreto | concrete pad |
| **plataforma de trabajo** | working deck |
| plataforma de trabajo elevadiza, plataforma para trabajo a varios niveles | elevating work platform |
| **plataforma de viga** | beam type platform |
| plataforma rodante | dolly |
| **plataforma rotatoria de trabajo** | rotating work platform |
| plataforma tipo escalera | ladder-type platform |
| **platillo, pestañas, brida** | flange |
| plato del plegador | beam head |
| **plató, altiplanicie** | plateau |
| plegadiza | folding |
| **pleno** | plenum |
| plomería [plo-me-RI-ya] | plumbing |
| **plomo** | lead, plumb bob |
| podadora de gasolina | reel power lawn mower |
| **podadora tipo arado** | sulky-type mower |
| podrido | rotten |

| | |
|---|---|
| polea | pulley |
| polea acanalada | sheave |
| polea inferior | boot pulley |
| polvo de algodón | cotton dust |
| polvo de algodón respirable sin borra | lint-free respirable cotton dust |
| polvo de asbesto | asbestos dust |
| polvo no depositado y suspendido en el aire | non deposited air-suspended powder |
| polvo relámpago | photographic flash powder |
| polvos | fines |
| polvos producidos al revestir con materia pulverizada | powder coating dust |
| poner en cortocircuito | short circuit |
| porta-filtro para la toma de muestra en el campo | field monitor cassette |
| portamangueras | hose rack |
| porta-neumáticos | tire rack |
| portillo giratorio de barrea doble | swivelled double-bar-gate |
| portón de cierre automático | self-closing, self-locking gate |
| poste | post |
| poste (andamio) | pole (scaffold) |
| poste-guía | guide post |
| prácticas ingenieriles, de | sound |

| | |
|---|---|
| **ingeniería correctas** | engineering practices |
| **pregunta [pre-GOON-ta]** | question (n) |
| **prensa de planchar** | flat work ironers |
| **prensa de tornillo** | vise |
| **prensa mecánica automática** | mechanical power-press |
| **prensas de forjar de platos accionados por gas comprimido** | high energy rate forming machine |
| **presión [pre-SYON]** | pressure |
| **presión de estallido calculada** | rated busting pressure |
| **presión de operación** | working pressure |
| **presión de prensado** | squeeze pressure |
| **presión establecida de servicio** | mark service pressure |
| **presión estática de la carga** | static head of the loading |
| **presión estática, carga estática** | static head |
| **presión hidrostática completa, cabezal hidrostático completo** | full hydrostatic head |
| **presión inicial** | opening pressure |
| **presión mecánica impelente, ventilación mecánica** | positive mechanical ventilation |

| | |
|---|---|
| presión por gravedad | gravity head |
| primera mano (de pintura) | undercoating |
| primeros auxilios | first aid |
| principio de gasómetro | gasometer principle |
| privilegio de antigüedad | seniority status |
| probador de circuitos | circuit tester |
| probadores | proofer |
| programa de detección | monitoring |
| programador de un recorrido completo | single stroke reset |
| prolongación del respaldo contra carga | load back rest extension |
| promedio de evaporación, razón de evaporación, tasa de evaporación | evaporation rate |
| propano [pro-PA-no] | propane |
| protección para la cabeza, protección para los pies | coverings (head, foot) |
| protector de esquinas | corner bead |
| protector de pintura | paint shield |
| protector de rodillas | knee pads |
| proyectil para indicar posición de impacto | spotting projectile |
| proyecto | project |
| prueba con martillo | hammer test |
| prueba de carga completa | dead-weight test |
| prueba de sonido por percusión | ring test |
| prueba de suelo, prueba de terreno, prueba de tierra | soil test |

| | |
|---|---|
| prueba visual | visual test |
| puente voladizo, madero saliente | outrigger ledger |
| puentear los fusibles | budging fuses |
| Puerta | eoor |
| puerta a prueba de fuego, puerta ignífuga | fire door |
| Puerta corrediza | sliding door |
| puerta de tranca | yard-arm-doorway |
| puerta de vaivén montada con bisagras hacia los lados | side linged swinging type door |
| puerta fabricada | Pre-hung door |
| puerta para limpieza | sludge door |
| puerto de vigilancia | view port |
| pulgada [pul-GA-da] | inch |
| pulgadas cuadradas | square inches |
| pulidora, afiladora, de superficie esmeriladora | surface grinder machine |
| pulir, lijar | buff |
| punto (punto gótico 14) | point (14 point gothic) |
| punto de agarre | bite |
| punto de apoyo | fulcrum point |
| punto de calibración | calibration point |
| punto de corte final, parada final | cut-off point |
| punto de desplazamiento | drift point |
| punto de enganche, de agarre | pinch point |

| | |
|---|---|
| **punto de llama, punto de inflamación** | flashpoint |
| **punto de sujeción** | prolongs anchor |
| **punto tipográfico** | point type |
| **punzadora** | punching |
| **que la máscara selle la cara** | face-piece-to-face seal |
| **queja [KE-ha], querella [ke-RE-ya], demanda [de-MAN-da], denuncia [de-NUN-sya], reclamo [re-KLA-mo]** | complaint |
| **quemador** | burner |
| **quemador de maleza** | weed burners |
| **querellante [ke-re-YAN-te], quejista [ke-HIS-ta]** | complainant |
| **químicos** | chemicals |
| **radio de recorrido** | swing radius |
| **radiografía del pecho** | chest roentgenogram |
| **raja** | crack (glass, porcelain) |
| **ranura** | slot |
| **ranura de extracción** | exhaust slot |
| **raspado** | grinding |
| **raspadora** | rasp |
| **rastrillo** | rake |
| **rebaba** | burr |
| **rebaje** | undercut |
| **rebanadoras de cuchilla de vaivén** | knife head of reciprocating |

| | blade slicers |
|---|---|
| **rebobinadora manual** | hand bailing machine |
| **recabado** | refinished |
| **recalcaduras** | upsetters |
| **receptáculo** | receptacle outlet |
| **receptáculo [re-sep-TA-ku-lo]** | outlet |
| **receptáculos de frente muerto** | dead front receptacles |
| **recinto, caja** | housing |
| **recipiente a presión** | pressure vessel |
| **recipiente de procesamiento** | process vessel |
| **recogida** | pickup (act of collecting) |
| **recolector del exceso de rocío seco** | dry type overspray collectors |
| **recolectores de polvo** | dust collection |
| **recortadora de chapa** | nibbler |
| **recoveco** | recess |
| **recto** | straight |
| **reductor** | reducer |
| **reemplazo de tejado** | re-roofing |
| **re-examen de mediados de temporada** | mid-season retest |
| **reflector de haz difuso** | floodlight |
| **reformación** | reshaping |
| **reforzamiento transversal** | cross bracing |
| **refrigerante** | refrigerant |

| | |
|---|---|
| refuerzo para techo | tar paper/roof underlayment |
| registro | cleanout |
| registro [re-HE-stro], pozo de registro | manhole |
| regla [REG-la] | rule, regulation |
| Regla metálica | straightedge |
| reglas substantivas | substantive rules |
| regulador de luz | dimmer |
| regulador del motor | motor controller |
| reja | railing (fence) |
| relevador, relé | relay |
| remache | rivet |
| remoción | removal |
| remolque | towing, trailer |
| remolque motorizado | truck crane |
| removedor de pintura | paint remover |
| rendimiento por hora | hourly rating |
| reparación | repair |
| repartidor de calefacción | heat exchanger |
| reponer | replenish |
| representante de los trabajadores / empleados [re-pre-sen-TAN-te de los tr-ba-DOR-es / em-ple-A-dos] | employee representative |
| representante del empleador [re-pre-sen-TAN-te del em-ple-A-dor], patrono [pat-RO-no], | employer |

| | |
|---|---|
| **patrón [pat-RON], jefe [HE-fe], empresario [em-pre-SAR-yo]** | |
| **representante laboral [re-pre-sen-TAN-te la-bor-AL]** | union representative |
| **reprogramación manual** | manual reset |
| **resguardo de contención, dique** | bulk head |
| **resguardo de rejilla** | grid guard |
| **resguardo mecánico, guarda para transmisión de energía** | mechanical power-transmission guard |
| **resguardo superior** | overhead guard |
| **resistencia** | resistance |
| **resistencia final** | ultimate strength |
| **resistencia mínima a la compresión** | minimum crushing strength |
| **respirador** | respirator |
| **respirador con purificador de aire motorizado** | powered air purifying respirator |
| **respirador con purificador de aire motorizado con filtro de gran eficacia para partículas** | powered air puriying respirator with high efficiency particulate filter |
| **respirador mecánico desechable con purificador** | single use air purifying |

| | |
|---|---|
| de aire | respirator |
| respirador mecánico desechable para polvo | single use dust respirator |
| respirador para polvo, respirador mecánico para polvo | dust respirator |
| respirador purificador de aire forzado | PAPR |
| respirador purificador de aire re-usable | reusable air purifying respirator |
| respirador que protege la nariz y la boca sin cubrir la barbilla | quarter mask |
| restauración | restoration |
| retén | detent |
| retenedores en los extremos | tie ends |
| revestimiento | coating |
| revestimiento | siding |
| revestimiento con dos elementos | dual component coating |
| revestimiento de las pestañas | flange facings |
| revestir con materia pulverizada | powder coating |
| ribete, borde | fringe |
| riesgo contra la salud [ri-ES-go KON-tra la sal-UD], peligro a la salud [pe-LI-gro a la sal-UD] | health hazard |
| riesgo(s) [ri-ES-go(s)], | hazard (s) |

| | |
|---|---|
| **peligro(s) [pe-LI-gro(s)]** | |
| **riesgos a la seguridad, peligros a la seguridad** | safety hazards |
| **rincón** | corner (inside) |
| **riostra, amarre** | brace |
| **rociado de manera arbitraria** | random spray |
| **rociador** | sprayer |
| **rocío** | spraying |
| **rocío por vapor** | steam blasting |
| **rodillo** | roller (paint) |
| **rodillo (pivotante / loco / de tensión de giro suave)** | smooth-pivoted idler role |
| **rodillo accionado** | drive roll |
| **rodillo activo** | live roll |
| **rodillo alimentador** | in-running roll |
| **rodillo de sujeción** | holddown roll |
| **rodillo para desprender** | stripping roll |
| **rodillo para la cara del edificio** | building face rollers |
| **rodillo-guía** | guide roller |
| **rueda** | wheel |
| **rueda central** | crown wheel |
| **rueda dentada** | sprocket |
| **rueda dentada de cadena, cadena montada** | chain sprocket |
| **rueda pivotante (loca), rueda de andamio rodante o movible** | caster |
| **ruido [Roo-EE-dough]** | noise |
| **ruido interrumpido** | impulsive noise |

| | |
|---|---|
| ruido por impacto | impact noise |
| saco de arena | sandbag |
| sacudidores o tambores para acondicionamiento | shakeout or conditioning tumbler |
| sal | salt |
| salida | exit |
| salida de descarga, salida final | exit discharge |
| salida, medios de salida | egress |
| salvar [sal-VAR], rescatar [res-ca-TAR] | rescue |
| secador | kiln |
| seguridad [se-gu-ri-DAD] | safety |
| selector de recorrido | stroking selector |
| sellador de horno | luterman |
| sello hermético al vapor | vapor-tight seal |
| separador | stripper |
| serpentín para calefacción por inducción | radiant heating coil |
| serrucho | handsaw |
| servicios de llamada desigual | call numbers uneven |
| sierra | saw |
| sierra alternativa | reciprocating saw, sawzall® |
| sierra alternativa, sierra de vaivén | sash gang saw |
| sierra circular | circular saw, skill saw |
| sierra coladora | jig saw |

| | |
|---|---|
| sierra con marco, serrucho para metal | hacksaw |
| sierra de contornear, sierra de marquetería | scroll saw |
| sierra de mano | handsaw |
| sierra de tronzar de alimentación manual y de mesa | hand-fed crosscut table saw |
| sierra de vaivén | saber saw |
| sierra eléctrica | saw, electric |
| sierra ingletadora, sierra de retroceso para ingletes | miter saw |
| sierra maestra | head saw |
| sierra múltiple | gang sam |
| sierras de cortar corredizas | sliding cut-off saws |
| sierras de cortar oscilantes | swing cut off saws |
| sifón | return bend, trap (plumbing) |
| sifón tipo P | P-trap |
| sifones | back siphonage |
| silenciador | muffler |
| sílice | silica (glass making) |
| silicona | silicone |
| sin aire, respiración entrecortada | breathlessness |
| sin residuos de petróleo (aire, nitrógeno, dióxido de carbono) | oil free (air, nitrogen, carbon |

| | |
|---|---|
| | dioxide) |
| **sin terminar** | unfinished |
| **Sindicato [sin-di-KA-to], unión [un-YON], unión laboral [un-YON la-bor-AL]** | union |
| **síntomas** | symptomatology |
| **sistema automático rociador** | automatic sprinkler system |
| **sistema de ángulo de inclinación** | sloping system |
| **sistema de barandas [sis-TE-ma de bar-AN-das]** | guardrail system |
| **sistema de columna de alimentación de agua** | wet standpipe system |
| **sistema de columna de alimentación de agua; vacío** | dry standpipe system |
| **sistema de conductor eléctrico** | electric runway conductor |
| **sistema de detención de caídas** | fall arrester |
| **sistema de formación de la sangre** | hematopoietic system |
| **sistema de inundación** | deluge system |
| **sistema de radio telefonía** | two-way voice communication system |
| **sistema de recuperación, sistema de recobrar** | retrieval system |

| | |
|---|---|
| sistema de rejas | grid |
| sistema de soporte | supporting systems |
| sistema de suspensión en ángulo | angulated roping |
| sistema para bombeo de concreto | pumpcrete system |
| sistemas de protección | protective systems |
| sobre ruedas, a móvil | mobile |
| sobre tierra, sobre el nivel | above grade |
| sobrecalentamiento | boilover |
| sofito | soffit |
| soga/cuerda | rope |
| soldador | welder |
| soldadura | welding |
| soldadura con cautín | soldered-brass |
| soldadura dura | brazing |
| soldadura dura de bronce | brazed-brass |
| soldadura dura o blanda, bronce-soldadura, cobre-soldadura, soldadura fuerte, soldadura con aleación de cobre | welding or brazing |
| soldadura por arco metálico protegido | shielding |
| soldadura por arco protegido por gas inerte | gas-shielded arc welding |
| soldadura por condensador | capacitor welding |
| soldadura por punto | spot welding |
| solera inferior | bottom plate |

| | |
|---|---|
| sonda | probe |
| sopladores, ventiladores, abanicos | blowers |
| soplar | blow down |
| soplete | torch (welding) |
| soporte | bearer |
| soporte | saddles |
| soporte de retención | supporting bearer |
| soporte del filtro | filler holder |
| soporte, escala de gancho, palometa de gancho | hook-over bracket |
| soportes | brackets |
| soportes de acero | supporting steel |
| soportes giratorios | trunnions |
| substancia química en polvo, químico en polvo | dry chemical |
| subterráneo | underground |
| suelo inestable, terreno inestable, | unstable soil |
| suelo, terreno tierra | soil |
| suelto | salary |
| sujetador de filtro abierto | open-face filter holder |
| sujetador tipo casquillo cuña | wedge socket type fastening |
| superficie de desgaste | wearing surface |
| tabla de capellada, pie, tablón de capellada | toeboard |

| | |
|---|---|
| tabla de concreto | concrete board |
| tabla de seguridad para apoyo | foot ladder board |
| tablero de servicio | service panel |
| tablón | plank |
| tablón con listones | chicken ladder |
| taladrar | boring |
| tallado de acero | zero cut |
| talladora | woodshaper |
| tamaño | size |
| tamaño bruto | rough size |
| tambor | tumbler |
| tambor elevado, tambor para levantar, elevar | hoisting drum |
| tambor exprimidor motorizado | engine drum extractor |
| tambor secador | drying can |
| tanque | kier |
| tanque a presión atmosférica | atmospheric tank |
| tanque de galvanización | galvanizing tank |
| tanque de recuperación | salvage tank |
| tanques con largueros | skid tank |
| tanques de carga motorizados; camión tanque | motor vehicle cargo tanks |
| tapa | cap |
| tapa | lid |
| tapa para respiradores, para ventilación | vent cap |
| tapa para respiradores, | vent piping |

| | |
|---|---|
| **tubería para ventilación** | |
| **tapa protectora de la válvula** | valve protecting cap |
| **tapajuntas** | flashing |
| **tapas a vapor** | steam jackets |
| **tapón** | plug (sink) |
| **tarugo, zoquete** | block (of wood) |
| **tasa de flujo, razón de flujo, medida del caudal** | flow rate |
| **tasa de resistencia al fuego** | fire resistance rating |
| **tazón** | bowl |
| **techado** | weather shelter |
| **techo** | ceiling |
| **techo abuhardillado** | gambrel roof |
| **techo flotante** | floating roof |
| **techo inclinado** | A-frame |
| **techo inclinado** | gable roof |
| **techo levadizo** | lifter roof |
| **teja de arcilla** | tile (roof) |
| **teja de asfalto** | shingle (asphalt) |
| **tejado** | roof |
| **-asfalto** | -asphalt |
| **-inclinado** | -gable |
| **-abuhardillado** | -gambrel |
| **-gotera** | -leak |
| **-a dos aguas** | -saddle (2 sided) |
| **-empizarrado** | -slate |
| **-de tejas** | |
| **-de estaño** | -tile |

| | -tin |
|---|---|
| **telar para anillos** | ring spinning frame |
| **temperaturas criogénicas** | cryogenic temperatures |
| **tenazas** | pliers (needle nose) |
| **tenazas** | tongs (large) |
| **tendencia a asentamiento por presión** | pressure-setting tendency |
| **tendido** | stringing |
| **tensión por tracción, tensión al halar o jalar** | pulling tension |
| **tensores** | turnbuckles |
| **terminal de la tubería de llenado** | filling pipe inlet terminal |
| **terminales de carga a granel** | bulk terminal |
| **terminales de goma deslizable/ajustable** | rubber slip end |
| **terminar con soldadura** | back welded |
| **terraza** | deck (outside) |
| **terreno blando** | soft material |
| **terreno en el que se cubre la basura con tierra** | sanitary land fill |
| **terreno inestable** | unstable material |
| **tierra** | dirt |
| **tijeras** | shears |
| **tijeras de aviación** | aviation snips |
| **tijeras para hojalata** | tin snips |

| | |
|---|---|
| tina | tub |
| tina de encolar | size box |
| tipo de flujo continuo | continuous flow type (flow mode) |
| tipo de suelo, tipo de terreno, tipo de tierra | soil type |
| tipo pica madera | woodpecker type |
| tipo ranura | slot-type |
| tira | strap |
| tirante de resorte | snap tie |
| tirantes | bracing |
| tiras | flooring strips |
| tiza | chalk |
| toalla | towel |
| tolva | hooper |
| tolva, bandeja, recipiente, caja, barril | bins |
| tolvas deflectoras | baffle type hoopers |
| toma de aire para combustión | combustion air inlet |
| toma de corriente | plug (electrical socket) |
| toma de fuerza directa | straight takeoff |
| toma de fuerza gradual | tapered takeoff |
| tomador de muestras | sampler |
| tomadores de prueba de copa abierta | open cup tester |
| tonel giratorio | blast cleaning |

| | |
|---|---|
| | barrel |
| **torcedor** | twister |
| **torcimiento** | warp |
| **tornillo de los terminales** | terminal screw |
| **tornillo, perno** | bolts |
| **tornillos o clavijas cónicas** | taper set |
| **torno sencillo** | whipline |
| **torre de andamio movible independiente** | free standing mobile scaffold tower |
| **torre de suministro de agua** | standpipe |
| **torsión** | torque |
| **trabajador (male) [tra-ba-ha-DOR]; / trabajadora (female) [tra-ba-ha-DOR-a]** | worker |
| **trabajador(es) [tra-ba-DOR / tra-ba-DOR-es], empleado(s) [em-ple-A-do(s), obrero(s) [o-BRE-ro(s)]** | employee (s) |
| **trabajadores en empleos no textiles** | non textile workers |
| **trabajo** | job |
| **trabajo de hojalatería** | body and fender work |
| **tracción lateral** | side pull |
| **tragaluz, claraboya** | skylight |
| **trampa** | trapdoor |
| **transformador** | transformer |
| **transistor** | transistor |
| **transmisión mecánica** | power- |

| | transmission |
|---|---|
| **transmisión y distribución de energía** | power transmission and distribution |
| **transportador** | conveyor |
| **trapo** | cloth, rag |
| **travesaño** | beam, bolster |
| **traviesa** | tie (framing) |
| **trazo** | layout |
| **tren de calibración para tomar muestra** | calibration sampling train |
| **trepadoras** | pole climbers |
| **trepadores para postes, dientes** | gaff |
| **tres conductores, tipo tres alambres** | three-wire type |
| **trinchador** | trencher |
| **trinchera [trin-CHE-ra], zanja [SAN-ha]** | trench |
| **trinquete** | ratchet |
| **triturador** | garbage disposer |
| **tronco protector** | brow log |
| **troquel** | die (power presses) |
| **troquel herramienta unificada** | unitized tooling |
| **tubería / línea flexible** | swing line |
| **tubería de plástico** | PVC pipe |
| **tubería de ventilación** | rent piping |
| **tubería, entubado,** | piping, tubing |

| | |
|---|---|
| accesorios, cañería, entubado | and fittings (hydrogen) |
| tuberías de extracción, tuberías de salida | withdrawal lines |
| tuberías de seguridad | safety relief lines |
| tubo | tube |
| tubo de descarga de la astilladora | chipper spout |
| tubo de descarga para gas | fuel gas outlet |
| tubo de llenado | fill stem |
| tubo de retorno | return pipe |
| tubo deslizable | slip tube |
| tubo en T | T-pipe |
| tubo flexible | swing pipe |
| tubos | pipes |
| tuercas | nuts |
| umbral | stop |
| unidad de ventana | window unit |
| unión giratoria | swivel joint |
| uniones del motor | motor couplings |
| uñas contra-rechazador | nonkick back fingers |
| uñas, anillos | lugs |
| urdidor | warper |
| usuario que mezcla explosivos o agentes detonantes | user-compounder |
| vaciado de emergencia | emergency disposal |

| | |
|---|---|
| vagones cisterna | rail tankcars |
| valle | valley |
| valor límite | limiting value |
| valor máximo | ceiling value |
| valor máximo | maximum peak |
| válvula | valve |
| válvula aprobada resistente a impacto | approved impact valve |
| válvula de cierre | shutoff valve |
| válvula de desagüe | waste valve |
| válvula de retención de flujo en retroceso | back-flow check valve |
| válvula de retención de resorte | spring laded check valve |
| válvula de seguridad | safety valve |
| válvula de seguridad accionada por piloto integrado | self-contained pilot operated relief valve |
| válvula de seguridad de contrapeso | weight-loaded relief valve |
| válvula de seguridad de tipo independiente con resorte | self-contained spring loader relief valve |
| válvulas de cierre | closure valves |
| válvulas de control remoto | remote valves |
| válvulas para la contrapresión | back pressure check valve |
| vaporizador | vaporizer-burner |
| vara de madera | wooden punch |
| vara para cargar | loading boom |
| varilla | rebar |

|  |  |
|---|---|
| varilla de embrague de seguridad | safety triprod |
| varilla, barra, vara (de conexión) | connecting rod |
| varillaje de sujeción individual | individual shackle rod |
| vástago de la válvula | valve stem |
| vatio | watt |
| vehículo de motor [ve-I-ku-lo de MO-tor] | motor vehicle |
| vehículo tanque | tank motor vehicle |
| velocidad de captura | capture velocity |
| velocidad de disparo del regulador, velocidad de desembrague del regulador | governor tripping speed |
| velocidad del aire centrípeto | inward air velocity |
| velocidad en el conducto | duct velocity |
| ventana | window |
| ventana de guillotina | sash window |
| ventilación cruzada | cross ventilation |
| ventilación mecánica, presión mecánica impelente | mechanical ventilation |
| ventilación para extracción | exhaust ventilation |
| ventilación, extracción | ventilation |
| ventilador | blower |
| ventilador | fan |

| | |
|---|---|
| vertical, afiladora vertical | vertical slip form |
| vestidor, ropero empotrado | walk-in closet |
| vestimenta que cubra el cuerpo | whole body clothing |
| vía | track |
| vibrador para hormigón, para concreto | concrete vibrators |
| vidriera | stain-glass window |
| viento de alambre | wire tie |
| viento de cuerda | tieback |
| viga de apoyo | runner |
| viga de espiga | needle beam |
| viga del plafón, viga de techo | ceiling beam |
| viga maestra de empalme | wood splice plates |
| viga principal | girder |
| viga separadora | spreader beam |
| viga transversal | cross beam |
| viga voladiza, viga saliente o que sobresale | outrigger beam |
| viga, travesaño | beam, rafter |
| viga, vigueta | joist |
| vigas doble T | eye beam |
| vigueta de acero | steel joist |
| vinilo | vinyl |
| viruta; paja de madera | excelsior |
| voltaje disruptivo | breakdown |
| voltio | volt |
| volumen de inspiración | maximal |

| | |
|---|---|
| **máxima** | inspiration volume |
| **zancos** | stilts |
| **zanja** | ditch |
| **zanjando; excavando** | trenching |
| **zapapico** | mattock |
| **zapata de guía** | guide shoe |
| **zarpa, cimiento** | footing |
| **zócalo** | baseboard |
| **zona de respiración** | breathing zone |

# Appendix I: Expressions

## Useful Spanish Expressions

| | |
|---|---|
| Please. | Por favor. |
| Thank you. | Gracias. |
| You're welcome. | De nada. |
| Excuse me | Disculpe |
| I need to see your driver's license? | Necesito ver su licencia de conductores. |
| How many years experience do you have in this profession? | ¿Cuántos años de experiencia tiene en esta profesión? |
| This job pays ($8,$9,$10,$11,$12, $13,$14) an hour. | Este trabajo se paga (ocho, nueve, diez, once, doce, trece, catorce) dólares por hora. |

# Key Expressions

| | |
|---|---|
| Excuse me, sir. | Perdón, señor. |
| Ma'am. | Señora. |
| Miss/Ms. | Señorita. |
| Do you speak English? | ¿Habla inglés? |
| Yes | Sí. |
| No. | No. |
| I don't speak a lot (of Spanish). Pay attention and listen to my instructions. | No hablo mucho (español). Preste atención y escuche mis instrucciones. |
| If you don't follow instructions, I will fire you. | Si no sigue instrucciones, le despediré. |
| Speak slower please. | Hable más despacio por favor. |
| Please repeat. | Repita por favor. |
| May I ask you a question? | ¿Puedo hacerle una pregunta? |

| | |
|---|---|
| Help me with this, right away. | Ayúdeme con esto, en seguida. |
| I'm the boss you are not. | Soy el patrón que usted no es. |
| A quality job is the only job we do. | Un trabajo de calidad es el único trabajo que hacemos. |
| If you break it, you buy it. | Si se le rompe, lo compra. |
| Treat all of the customer's property and personal belongings with respect. | Respete todas pertenencias y efectos personales del cliente. |
| Don't be careless. Put all tools back where they belong. | No seas una persona descuidada. Coloque las herramientas en su lugar correcto. |
| Pick up the pace or go home. | Apúrense o váyase a casa. |

# Measurements

| Inches | Pulgadas |
|--------|----------|
| Feet | Pies |
| 1/16 | Un dieciseisavo |
| 1/8 | Un octavo |
| ¼ | Un cuarto |
| ½ | Media (pulgada) |
| ¾ | Tres cuartos |
| 3' 8½" | Tres pies ocho y media pulgadas |

**For example:**

**Cut me a piece that is 48" x 59".**

**Córteme una pieza de cuarenta y ocho pulgadas por cincuenta y nueve pulgadas.**

# Appendix III: Numbers

| | |
|---|---|
| 1 uno | 21 veintiuno |
| 2 dos | 22 veintidós |
| 3 tres | 23 veintitrés |
| 4 cuatro | 24 veinticuatro |
| 5 cinco | 25 veinticinco |
| 6 seis | 26 veintiséis |
| 7 siete | 27 veintisiete |
| 8 ocho | 28 veintiocho |
| 9 nueve | 29 veintinueve |
| 10 diez | 30 treinta |
| | |
| 11 once | 31 treinta y uno |
| 12 doce | 32 treinta y dos |
| 13 trece | 33 treinta y tres..... |
| 14 catorce | |
| 15 quince | 40 cuarenta |
| 16 dieciséis | |
| 17 diecisiete | 50 cincuenta |
| 18 dieciocho | 60 sesenta |
| 19 diecinueve | 70 setenta |
| 20 veinte | 80 ochenta |
| | 90 noventa |
| | |
| | 100 cien |
| | |
| | 1000 mil |
| | |
| | 1.000.000 un millón |

# SEAMLESS SOLUTIONS, LLC.
# NEW YORK

**Copyright ©2013**
**Seamless Solutions, LLC**
**ISBN 978-0615757636**
**All Rights Reserved.**

65940618R00130

Made in the USA
Lexington, KY
29 July 2017